Decolonizing Environmentalism

Decolonizing Environmentalism

Alternative Visions and Practices of Environmental Action

Prakash Kashwan and Aseem Hasnain

BLOOMSBURY ACADEMIC
LONDON · NEW YORK · OXFORD · NEW DELHI · SYDNEY

BLOOMSBURY ACADEMIC
Bloomsbury Publishing Plc
50 Bedford Square, London, WC1B 3DP, UK
1385 Broadway, New York, NY 10018, USA
29 Earlsfort Terrace, Dublin 2, Ireland

BLOOMSBURY, BLOOMSBURY ACADEMIC and the Diana logo are
trademarks of Bloomsbury Publishing Plc

First published in Great Britain 2025

A catalogue record for this book is available from the British Library.

Library of Congress Cataloging-in-Publication Data
Names: Kashwan, Prakash, author. | Hasnain, Aseem, author.
Title: Decolonizing environmentalism : alternative practices and visions for
environmental action / Prakash Kashwan, Aseem Hasnain.
Description: New York : Bloomsbury Academic, 2025. |
Includes bibliographical references and index.
Identifiers: LCCN 2024019580 (print) | LCCN 2024019581 (ebook) |
ISBN 9781350335479 (hardback) | ISBN 9781350335462 (paperback) |
ISBN 9781350335486 (epub) | ISBN 9781350335493 (ebook)
Subjects: LCSH: Environmentalism–Social aspects. | Environmentalism–Citizen
participation. | Indigenous peoples–Social conditions.
Classification: LCC GE195 .K37 2025 (print) | LCC GE195 (ebook) |
DDC 363.7–dc23/eng/20240429
LC record available at https://lccn.loc.gov/2024019580
LC ebook record available at https://lccn.loc.gov/2024019581

ISBN: HB: 978-1-3503-3547-9
       PB: 978-1-3503-3546-2
     ePDF: 978-1-3503-3549-3
    eBook: 978-1-3503-3548-6

Typeset by Integra Software Services Pvt. Ltd.
Printed and bound in Great Britain

To find out more about our authors and books visit www.bloomsbury.com
and sign up for our newsletters.

To environmental justice defenders who fight and sacrifice for a socially just and ecologically thriving planet.

Contents

Figures

DECOLONIZING ENVIRONMENTALISM

Alternative Practices and Visions for Environmental Futures

Prakash Kashwan
Aseem Hasnain

Prakash Kashwan is Associate Professor of Environmental Studies at Brandeis University. He is also the Chair of the Environmental Justice concentration in the Master of Public Policy program at the Heller School of Social Policy and Management. Kashwan is the author of *Democracy in the Woods: Environmental Conservation and Social Justice in India, Tanzania, and Mexico* (Oxford University Press 2017), the editor of *Climate Justice in India* (Cambridge University Press 2022), one of the editors of the journal *Environmental Politics* (Taylor & Francis), and co-founder of Climate Justice Network.

Aseem Hasnain is Assistant Professor of Sociology at California State University, Fresno. He is interested in politics and culture and their ideological dimensions. His research engages with race/caste, labor, social movements, and their connections with capitalism and colonialism. Aseem grew up in Lucknow, India, and lives in Fresno, California.

Unpacking Mainstream Environmentalism: Heroic and Mundane

Lisa Curtis is a star millennial, a politics and environment studies major, green entrepreneur, and founding CEO of Kuli Kuli. She sells Moringa to health-conscious consumers, with the intention of improving the well-being of smallholder women farmers who are Kuli Kuli's main suppliers. Lisa conceived Kuli Kuli, a new-age, planet-friendly sustainable enterprise, during her time with the Peace Corps in Niger. She volunteered in a village health center, acquiring valuable understanding of nutritional challenges in West African villages, and how the Indigenous species of Moringa trees could help address them. Kuli Kuli is a Certified B Corp, which sources its raw material from small family farms that meet high standards of environmental performance and public transparency.[1]

Lisa's story is an inspiration for millennials. She was a Udall Scholar, was in the Forbes 30 Under 30 leaders list, and was celebrated by the Muhammad Ali Center as a "dedicated humanitarian." Despite these credentials, Lisa does not like to be called an environmentalist, a term she argues "has been sort of corrupted ... politicized." She calls herself a "social entrepreneur" instead, while avoiding words like "environment," "earth," and "climate change" in her company's mission statement. Lisa Curtis's story resonates with many millennials who do not want to be labeled environmentalists, even though they actually think and act as environmentalists.[2]

Thomas Hayden, professor of environmental communication at Stanford, is familiar with these anxieties. To him, the millennial takes on environmentalism feel very different from that of his youth, thirty years ago. Hayden says he used to sport "white-guy-dreadlocks" and lived in a commune called the Eco-House, a label that many US colleges have adopted for "living learning communities." Comparing the environmentalism of his youth and the millennials' perspective on it, Hayden said, "even I cringe a little remembering it." Hayden's reflections raise questions about the essence of US environmentalism of the 1970s and 1980s. How rebellious was it then and what became of it over time? In pursuit of an answer, we will take you on a detour into the history of contemporary environmentalism. In the following section, we trace important continuities and tensions between the environmentalism then versus the environmentalism now. This is followed by a discussion of a few famous environmentalists and their actions to reflect on the promises and pitfalls of the phenomenon of heroic environmentalism. We conclude this chapter by introducing key arguments of this book about the intellectual foundations of contemporary environmentalism in Euro-American societies and lay down ways forward for decolonizing environmentalism.

Environmentalism in the West: A Trajectory

Major environmental crises during the 1960s—including the Santa Barbara oil-well blowout in California and the Cuyahoga River in Cleveland, Ohio, catching fire—were instrumental in catapulting environmental issues into American public consciousness. The publication of Rachel Carson's *Silent Spring* in 1968 and nation-wide celebrations of the first Earth Day in April 1970 fueled public advocacy on the environment and pressured politicians. Powerful corporations afraid of public mobilization and stringent environmental policies swung into action. However, instead of opposing environmental regulations openly, as climate change deniers did until recently, they ran covert operations to dilute environmental discourses. A hugely popular public service announcement (PSA), "Crying Indian," that ran on national TV from 1971 to the late 1980s offers an interesting insight into these machinations. Picture this:

> Iron Eyes Cody, an actor in Native American garb, paddles a birch bark canoe on water that seems, at first, tranquil and pristine, but that becomes increasingly polluted along his journey. He pulls his boat ashore and walks toward a bustling freeway. As the lone Indian ponders the polluted landscape, a passenger hurls a paper bag out a car window. The bag bursts on the ground, scattering fast-food wrappers all over the Indian's beaded moccasins. In a stern voice, the narrator comments: "Some people have a deep, abiding respect for the natural beauty that was once this country. And some people don't." The camera zooms in on Iron Eyes Cody's face to reveal a single tear falling, ever so slowly, down his cheek.[3]

Crying Indian is often cited among the most memorable and influential advertisements in the history of television. It was run so often that TV stations had to frequently replace the tapes. For many Americans, "the Crying Indian became the quintessential symbol of environmental idealism." Most Americans, however, did not realize that the "Crying Indian" PSA was sponsored by beverage companies to undermine environmental groups that were seeking to hold industry groups responsible for the proliferation of disposable items that triggered the solid waste crisis.

Heather Rogers's book, *Gone Tomorrow: The Hidden Life of Garbage,* demonstrates that corporations sponsored and coordinated this counter-mobilization through a charity called Keep America Beautiful (KAB), founded in 1953. By 1960, the KAB had launched what turned out to be a half-century-long partnership with the Ad Council in the United States. "Crying Indian" and KAB, which continues to be active even today, were designed to individualize responsibility for environmental problems. It successfully diverted Americans' attention away from a much bigger environmental problem, that is, huge quantities of solid waste resulting from the production and consumption of goods sold by these corporations.[4]

The backers of "Crying Indian" included the American Can Co., the Owens-Illinois Glass Co., Coca-Cola, and the Dixie Cup Co., who did not make the information about their sponsorship public. "Crying Indian" was a "public relations campaign that exploited public sentiments toward environmental protection to deflect attention from the wasteful practices in the beverage and packaging industry."[5] However, their pretense of environmentalism became apparent when KAB leadership decried numerous "Bottle Bills" that would require beverage producers to sell their products in reusable containers. In one case, KAB leaders sought to discredit advocates of Bottle Bills by referring to them as "communists."

Dr. Suess's iconic 1971 best-seller, *The Lorax*, reinforced the tendency to individualize responsibility for environmental care and protection. *The Lorax* remains popular to date, with its most popular slogan transformed into a meme: "Unless someone like you cares a whole awful lot, nothing is going to get better." While mass awareness of environmental protection is necessary, it is not sufficient to cope with the severity of environmental and climate crises. These civilizational challenges cannot be addressed without system-wide transformative changes.

Considering the ongoing youth mobilization around environmental and climate justice, readers may wonder about the merits of our interest in a deep exploration of the individualization of environmental care. We engage with youth climate movements like Greta Thunberg-led Fridays for Future in later chapters and applaud them for broadening the ambit of their demands. However, environmental and climate justice movements are still not adequately represented within mainstream environmentalism in industrially advanced countries. The popular understanding of environmental and climate change policies in such nations continues to focus on sustainable consumption and on building renewable energy infrastructure. In a recent survey of over 15,000 individuals in the United States and Europe, plastic waste—linked to individual consumption—polled much higher than other deeper environmental problems, such as "loss of biodiversity" and "depletion of natural resources."[6] In fact, between 2000 and 2023, Americans' concern about "loss of tropical rain forests" has declined by more than 10 percentage points. More worryingly, the support for environmental protection has become increasingly partisan in the United States.[7] These statistics look very different in Europe; 94 percent of Europeans say that "protecting the environment is important to them personally." Over 70 percent of Europeans want the EU, national governments, and corporations to do more to protect the environment. Yet, the most popular environmental solutions remain individual actions: 66 percent "Separated most of their waste for recycling," 45 percent "Avoided single-use plastic goods other than plastic bags or bought reusable plastic products," and 42 percent "Bought local products."[8] Overall, environmentally responsible consumption, recycling, and other types of individual environmental actions are the most relatable environmental topics for people in industrially advanced countries.

The valorization of individual responsibility has engendered a unique variety of environmentalism in Euro-American societies. These variants are centered on heroic battles waged by highly motivated individuals such as Erin Brockovich, Jane Goodall, and Robert Bilott, among others. The phenomenon of heroic environmentalism has been and continues to be popular among Americans, especially in Hollywood blockbusters. The 2019 legal thriller *Dark Waters* celebrates the heroic battle that Robert Bilott waged and won single-handedly against DuPont that subjected an entire West Virginia community to untreated toxic waste. Another widely known name is environmental activist Erin Brockovich, who mobilized residents of Hinkley, CA, against the Pacific Gas and Electric Company in 1993. This led to the largest payout ever awarded for a direct-action lawsuit, making Brockovich a hero, and later the lead character in an Oscar-winning Julia Roberts starrer.[9] What is it about heroic environmentalism that makes it so appealing and popular? In the next section, we look beyond the headlines to map out the history and implications of heroic environmentalism.

The Attraction and Limits of
Heroic Environmentalism

Rachel Carson is credited for the origins of modern American environmentalism. Often introduced as a writer, marine biologist, environmentalist, and a naturalist, Rachel warned against the dangers of environmental pollution.[10] Linda Lear, Carson's authoritative biographer, introduces her as "the finest nature writer of the Twentieth Century ..." Like Lear, most commentators have portrayed Carson as a "nature writer" while actively erasing the political dimensions of her environmental activism. The author of a Rachel Carson profile published in the *New Yorker* heavily criticized an anthology highlighting the far-reaching political impact of *Silent Spring*, arguing that "Political persuasion is a strange measure of the worth of a piece of prose whose force lies in knowledge and wonder."[11] To talk of political *persuasion* is an understatement of the significant influence that Carson had in motivating the overhaul of environmental regulations in the United States. This includes the National Environmental Policy Act (1969), the establishment of the Environmental Protection Agency in 1970, the Clean Water Act (1972), and the Endangered Species Act (1972). Carson's advocacy also contributed to the enactment of the Toxic Substances Control Act of 1976, which gave the EPA authority to regulate or ban all six compounds indicted in *Silent Spring*—DDT, chlordane, heptachlor, dieldrin, aldrin, and endrin.[12]

Carson's intent to hold the industry and military accountable for the use of chemicals is erased out of most narratives about her work. The individualization of Rachel Carson started with vilification campaigns by sympathizers of pesticides and chemical industries. A reviewer writing for *Time* magazine framed her writing as "emotion-fanning" and her arguments "unfair, one-sided, hysterically overemphatic, and inaccurate outburst."[13] The celebration of Carson's work in popular culture also selectively reinforced the image of an individual hero fighting for nature. A country song by Billy Jonas, Ellis Paul, and Sharon Teeler exemplifies such individualization:

> And oh, they're tearing the big trees down
> They're covering the crops with a cloud of spray
> And the bulldozers and the high-rises from town
> Come so close you can't hear the forest sounds
> Rachel wrote a book on an old typewriter
> About the poison in the atmosphere
> And in the air we breathe
> She told the truth and the world started listening
> She was talking for the animals
> Speaking for the trees[14]

Carson's work is wrapped up in the mystique of her "talking for the animals and speaking for the trees." The individualization of Carson's environmentalism is ironic, given that her most important contribution was to mobilize public opinion for holding industry and the state accountable. As a group of high school students who prepared an informative web resource on Rachel Carson's contributions say, "Carson's willingness to lead in the effort to expose the harms of pesticides meant *a campaign against powerful industries, the government, and public opinion. Silent Spring was revolutionary; it shattered the misconception that man and nature were separate entities.*"[15] Yet, the dominant impulses of individualism within American literary and cultural milieu ended up depoliticizing her work and reduced it to an individual's fight for nature.

Carson is not an exception though—virtually every American environmental icon is presented as an extraordinary individual who fought to protect nature against the ravages of humanity. This list is topped by Jane Goodall, a grandmotherly Rockstar celebrity who is worshipped by the younger generation for her lifelong commitment to protecting critically endangered chimpanzees. In June 2010, the *Guardian* published an interview with Goodall to celebrate the fiftieth anniversary of her discovery of Chimpanzee's use of tools, which was believed until then to be a skill known only to humans. The first thing Goodall did after this marvelous discovery was to telegraph her employer, the British Paleontologist Louis Leakey (father of renowned wildlife conservationist Richard Leakey). Louis's response registered young Jane Goodall as a prominent figure in the history of science: "Now we must redefine man, redefine tools, or accept chimpanzees as humans."[16] It is unfortunate though that the quest never turned into one about the unity between humans and other species. Instead, Jane Goodall and other conservationists have inadvertently promoted a view of nature as an exotic thing—something that exists outside human society. Karen Kabo, an American novelist, writes in her book *In Praise of Difficult Women*:

> As a child, I idolized her. Jane Goodall, "the girl who lived among the wild chimpanzees," was blond and looked smart in her khaki shorts as she walked on thick jungle branches in her bare feet and play-wrestled with baby chimps. I'd seen her in National Geographic, which I would avidly page through before I could even read. We lived in the L.A. suburbs, and even though we had a swimming pool, I was aware that my life was sadly lacking in adventure.[17]

Exoticizing pristine nature reinforces the celebrity of Goodall and helps shape young environmentalists who are charmed by wild

"African adventures" afforded to privileged Europeans and Americans. Individual heroism runs deep within the dominant strands of environmentalism, especially in the Global North. These tendencies stand out further in the case of another celebrity environmentalist, Robert Hunter, cofounder of Greenpeace. An obituary celebrating his contributions in the *Times* referred to the phenomenon as "personal environmental activism."

Perhaps no other group has done more to fuse together the personal and militant dimensions of environmentalism than Greenpeace, which trains "ecowarriors" to "mind bomb" potential supporters with ghastly images of environmental destruction. These are extremely effective tools, as evident from the deep impressions they leave on college students.[18] One such class discussion was organized around a Greenpeace video on how the cosmetics giant Dove's sourcing of palm oil contributes to the destruction of peatlands and orangutans in Indonesian rainforests. This video centers on a young Indonesian girl, whose life chances are being harmed by rapacious demands for the natural resource attributed to Dove's best-selling cosmetics. Featuring a young Indonesian girl as the main subject is an especially powerful response to Dove's portrayal of its cosmetics as a means for women's empowerment, a trend that is sometimes labeled as "femvertising."[19] Greenpeace also travels the farthest in its support for the protection of the rights of Indigenous and rural communities in their struggles for environmental stewardship. At the same time, some North American Greenpeace activists, including "Eco-huntress" Emily Hunter, continue to promote "personal environmental activism" as the coolest form of environmental responsibility, undermining the critical role of collective action.[20]

Canadian environmental scholar Peter Dauvergne offers a fundamental critique of such heroic individual environmentalism— both the peaceful variety practiced by the likes of Jane Goodall and the direct-action style of Greenpeace and Sea Shepherd.[21] In *Environmentalism of the Rich*, Dauvergne argues that as commendable as such heroic actions may be, they rarely ignite large-scale mass environmental conservation movements. Moreover, heroic environmentalism does not confront the "politics of producing (and desiring) ever-more wealth and consumption ... alter the forces of exploitation or inequality ... [or] reduce the overall consequences of consumption."[22] Heroic personal environmentalism prioritizes the interests and concerns of privileged individuals, big corporations, and powerful states. For example, it relies on a number of privileges that activists from industrially advanced countries enjoy, especially when they take their environmentalism to countries in the Global South. On the contrary, local environmental activists in such nations are at much greater risk. They fight environmental degradation often at the cost of their safety.

More than 1,900 environmental defenders were murdered between 2012 and 2022 across the globe.[23] Berta Cáceres was one of these brave defenders. A Honduran Indigenous leader, co-founder of the National Council of Popular and Indigenous Organizations of Honduras (COPINH), Berta was a winner of the Goldman Environmental Prize, 2015. Berta mobilized her community and transnational solidarities against the infrastructure developers supported by international financial organizations, which threatened territorial rights of her Lenca communities.

In March 2016, Berta was assassinated for her decade-long fight against a project to build the Agua Zarca Dam.[24] Murders, maiming, and assassinations of local environmental activists are rampant across the Global South.[25] Unlike them, environmental heroes and warriors from the Global North enjoy unprecedented support, media attention, and the option to return to safety when they choose.

Personal environmental activism in formerly colonized countries also runs the risk of reinforcing neocolonial inequalities. A case in point is American occupational therapist-turned primatologist Diane Fossey, who stretched "heroic environmentalism" to its worst extreme. Fossey was notorious for her vigilante approach to protecting Gorillas

Figure 1 Bertha Zuniga Caceres, daughter of Bertha Caceres (Honduran Indigenous environmental defender) speaks at a rally after her mother's assassination.

Photo: Daniel Cima/COPINH/flickr/cc.

in the Virunga mountains of Rwanda. Fossey aggressively tracked and chased *alleged* poachers all the way back to their villages. In one case, she ripped the roof from an alleged poacher's hut and set it on fire. On another occasion, she kidnapped an alleged poacher's child as a form of punishment. In yet another bizarre incident, Fossey shot dead thirty heads of cattle found grazing close to the Gorilla reserve.[26] In a letter to a friend, Fossey even boasted about torturing a poacher, "We stripped him and spread eagled him and lashed the holy blue sweat out of him with nettle stalks and leaves …"[27] Amy Vedder of the Yale School of Forestry & Environmental Studies, a close associate of Fossey, says that Fossey's "hostility and mistrust toward the Rwandans" made her "extremely dismissive of them." Even an otherwise sympathetic report celebrating Fossey's devotion to Gorilla conservation states that she "met all Africans with condescendence and rejection."[28]

Fossey's racist vigilantism, however, was not just tolerated, but celebrated by conservationists and popular media. National

Geographic, BBC, and other Western media outlets honored her with headlines, such as "The Renegade Scientist Who Taught Us to Love Gorillas" and "The woman who gave her life to save the Gorillas."[29] *Vanity Fair* quoted Fossey's former colleague who defended her, claiming that "It wasn't that she was a racist, she just disliked human beings."[30] Such excuses are difficult to sustain given encounters recounted by multiple colleagues and witnesses. There seems to be a broad consensus that she despised ordinary Rwandans, who were dispossessed of their traditional homelands when wildlife reserves were carved out under the influence of Western conservation models and policies.[31] Fossey certainly valued Gorillas more than Rwandan people for whom she used the racist slur "wogs."[32] Perhaps most damaging of all, *Washington Post* reported, "Because the [alleged] poachers were Black, she forbade her African trackers from approaching too close in an effort to keep the Gorillas wary of Black faces."[33]

Diane Fossey was one of the white colonists who treated wildlife reserves in African nations as their personal fiefdoms. Yet, such repulsive forms of heroic environmentalism are rewarded with adulation from environmentally conscious individuals. Unless they become aware of its deeply colonial and racist background, it is difficult for most sympathizers to fathom the negative consequences of heroic environmentalism. In the absence of criticism of heroic environmentalism, sympathizers are motivated even more strongly to do what they can individually. The narratives and imagery of heroic individual environmentalism create opportunities for market-based environmentalism. It makes individuals believe that environmentally conscious shopping decisions are a way of expressing solidarity with heroic environmentalists. We call this form of environmentalism, expressed through green consumerism and other market-based practices, "mundane environmentalism."

Mundane Environmentalism and the Market

In April 2015 Starbucks announced that 99 percent of its supply chain had been verified as ethically sourced. Starbucks became the largest coffee retailer to achieve this milestone, for which it had been working with one of the largest and most influential global conservation groups, Conservation International.[34] Starbucks celebrates this important milestone on September 9 (9/9) at its stores across the globe. The company nudges customers to feel proud of their sustainable coffee purchases. Baristas write "99" on customers' cups and host mini-seminars to educate them on Starbucks's ethical practices that benefit coffee farmers, most of them in the Global South.[35] This is not a one-off annual marketing gimmick, though.

Starbucks also collaborates with the Costa Rican Coffee Institute (ICAFE) and has developed a blueprint for transparent and sustainable sourcing, benefiting more than a million farmers and workers around the world.[36] Moreover, Starbucks announced its intent to broaden the scope of its ethical supply chain to an estimated 25 million people across the globe who grow coffee for their livelihood.[37] It also committed to investing $50 million to help farmers renovate their farm or pursue more sustainable practices. As a founding member of the Sustainable Coffee Challenge, Starbucks collaborates with other actors in the industry to make coffee "the world's first sustainable agricultural product." All in all, Starbucks has invested more than $100 million in supporting coffee communities through collaborative farmer programs, farmer support centers, farmer loans, and forest carbon projects. Starbucks is also spearheading several Collective Action Networks, including one to replace and replant 1 billion coffee plants.

Environmental activists have scrutinized these claims. Treehugger. com ran a fact check on Starbucks's green claims. It suggests that the Starbucks-sponsored *Coffee and Farmer Equity Practices,* which goes by the acronym CAFÉ, encourages and rewards shade-grown coffee, but doesn't require it.[38] Shade-grown coffee has a much lower environmental footprint with additional benefits, such as conserving habitat, preserving soil quality, and needing less pesticides. Similarly, Starbucks' *Million Coffee Trees* campaign has been challenged by groups such as the Stand (formerly ForestEthics), which estimates that Starbucks was responsible for the logging of 1.6 million trees to meet its annual demand of 4 billion disposable coffee cups.[39]

Despite these concerns, Starbucks is a leader among environmentally friendly businesses. Being headquartered in Seattle adds to the company's progressive credo and its overall popularity among coffee-sipping environmentalists. Starbucks is but one of the hundreds of multinational corporations and thousands of smaller start-ups and enterprises that seek to integrate environmentally conscious or ethical consumption, sustainability, and social justice into their business operations. The popularity of environmentally conscious products and green consumerism relies on the notion that markets can be an important solution for the challenges of environmental protection and climate change. These claims have huge appeal because they create opportunities for responsible consumption, though at a premium.

Popular concepts such as sustainability seemingly include broader concerns about the exploitation of the environment and people, but, as we show in the following pages, they have severe limitations. Even the most radical sustainability initiatives often boil down to individualization of environmental responsibility and action without addressing core issues such as hyper consumption and production. We will carefully examine the efficacy of sustainability and market-based environmentalism in the next chapter. For now, we underline that market-based environmentalism rewards individual effort at the cost of collective action and systemic change, while sustaining higher consumption. In this sense, market-based solutions ensure the perpetuation of individualistic environmentalism, which has failed to respond to the scale of environmental challenges we confront today.

Data from Copernicus, the European Union's climate and weather monitoring service, shows that calendar year 2023 was 1.52°C hotter on average than temperatures before industrialization, which scientists consider to be a critical climate tipping point.[40] Another team of scientists have reported alarming new findings about soil temperatures. They found that the intensity of heat extremes is increasing 0.7°C per decade faster in the soil than in air near the surface.[41] Another record shattered just as we prepare to send this book to the press. In February 2024, the ocean surface measured 69.91°F (21.06°C) on average worldwide, a record high, which led to the Great Barrier Reef undergoing its fifth mass bleaching in eight years.[42] What's worse? Climate crisis is only one aspect of the broader environmental crisis. Scientists show that the planetary system has transgressed six of the nine planetary boundaries, which demarcate Earth's safe operating space for humanity.[43] Mainstream environmentalism has failed on its own terms. It needs a radical overhaul.

Toward Decolonizing Environmentalism

The coinciding of inter-related crises of social and economic inequalities, democratic backsliding, environmental degradation, and climate breakdown—sometimes referred to as a "polycrisis"— demands reflections about not only the efficacy of mainstream environmentalism but also the foundational ideas on which mainstream environmentalism is built. The present moment is rife with significant uncertainties but also with the potential for transformative change. Proposals for moving forward, however, are divided between two distinct approaches. The first approach is premised on the power of markets, individual responsibility, and high-tech solutions to see us through these crises, without accounting for their root causes in imperialism, colonialism, profiteering, and domination. Proponents of technical solutions to the climate crisis barely acknowledge the ongoing legacies of these processes—the endless extraction of resources and humans, consumerism, and the discriminatory ways in which vulnerable communities have been sacrificed in the pursuit of economic development. In some cases, despite acknowledging these painful outcomes, techno-managerial solutions remain blind to and risk reinforcing persisting neocolonial and capitalist inequalities. Such techno-managerial solutions are popular among corporations, philanthropic trusts, government agencies, well-known names in science and technology, and the mainstream media. They use confident, simplistic, positive language wrapped in packets of assurance and comfort. The proposals for geoengineering that we discuss later in this book promise to tackle climate crisis through Star Wars-style fantasies. Techno-managerial approaches seem very persuasive in a world where time is short, multi-tasking is the norm, buzzwords galore, and where deep thinking is often replaced by the high adrenaline blitzkrieg on social media platforms.

The second approach to environmentalism offers a critical, history-conscious, and politically engaged way for addressing the root causes of the climate crisis, without presenting dazzling yet simplistic solutions. Proponents of this approach ask fundamental questions about the relations that have historically bound humans, non-humans, nature, space, and time in complex webs, how these webs were ruptured, and how to repair them for a healthier and inclusive future. This approach draws from big-picture thinkers like Achille Mbembe, Amitav Ghosh, Dina Gilio-Whitaker, Kyle Whyte, and Dorceta Taylor who have shone a spotlight on the root causes of our present-day environmental and climate crisis, and public-minded scholars like Julian Agyeman, Farhana Sultana, Robin Wall

Kimmerer, and Femi Taiwo who seek to bridge academic research and popular debates. This approach also includes scholars who go the extra mile to assess the effects of policies and programs for vulnerable communities, researchers who test the veracity of shiny policies and initiatives, activists who have cut their teeth fighting for justice, and communities that have bravely pushed back against profit-hungry corporations that have bulldozed the environment and anyone who dares to stand in their way. These communities challenge big businesses and their partners in governments, media, and the non-profit world. These activists and writers demand a fundamental transformation of economy, society, and structures of international governance that have pushed us into the horrors of a polycrisis. They refuse to imagine climate action as a VR video game that one can play fantasizing solutions that blend seamlessly into entertainment. These thinkers, public intellectuals, scholars, and activists offer a slow, reflexive, difficult but realistic pathway to a just future.

Despite the rich scholarship from humanities and some parts of social sciences, these ideas have yet to feed back into rethinking of the foundations of mainstream environmentalism. A part of this has to do with the nature of humanities scholarship, which offers deep philosophical arguments, without necessarily wading into specific elements of praxis. As a result, as Indigenous scholars have warned, in many cases, decolonization has been reduced to a "metaphor."[44] Similarly, colonialism is often reduced, quite erroneously, to a historical phenomenon, the pre-capitalist stage of human societies.[45] In this book, we seek to build on rich insights from critically oriented scholarship and deeply engaged activism to inform a radical rethinking of mainstream environmentalism. We also invite you to engage with the transformative visions that are grounded in tried-and-true grassroots actions, which we translate into broader political and institutional strategies. This multi-faceted perspective we offer on radical activism, which is engaged simultaneously with grassroots and higher-level institutions and strategies, is crucially important and insufficiently developed in the debates on decolonization. The chapters ahead are meant to facilitate these reflections and pave pathways for dealing with contemporary crises in a just and effective manner.

Our first main argument is that mainstream environmentalism is based on a Eurocentric worldview which privileges the values, ideas, norms, practices, and interests of industrially advanced countries, with a very strong emphasis on individual choices and the inevitability of market-based solutions. In Chapter 2, we show how these dynamics work within dominant approaches to the environment and climate. We grapple with the deceptive notion of the "end of colonialism," by brainstorming the long-term consequences of "Colonization of the Mind." We show how power and inequalities within the Global South reinforce the age-old hierarchies between Global North and South. These inequalities appear in how powerful scientific and policy communities imagine the risks of speculative climate technologies, such as solar geoengineering and carbon dioxide removal, which is the focus of Chapter 3. We demonstrate how the Western-speak for risk-risk trade-offs in planetary-scale technological solutions may distribute risks along historically patterned global inequalities, especially on communities in the Global South.

In Chapter 4, we show how these values manifest in the popular understanding of green consumerism and sustainability. Yet, the influence of Eurocentrism is not limited to individualistic values and practice. Instead, Eurocentric thinking is part of an entire system that is part of much longer histories and larger contemporary geographies of colonialism and capitalism. The arguments we make in this book apply to a broad set of societies, including those that were never formally colonized or where settler colonization masquerades as "discovery" of the new world, such as in the United States.

Our second argument tackles the paradoxical failures coming from a lack of critical reflections within mainstream environmentalism despite the popularity of Indigenous environmentalism. Amid the din of technocratic solutions, vigorous and sustained pushbacks from scholars and activists for the recognition of rights of Indigenous and other frontline communities have become a standard reference in policy debates on climate change and the environment. Yet, as we discuss in Chapter 5, barring a few exceptions, such recognition often simplifies Indigenous knowledge as an instrument for the pursuit of goals defined by Euro-American environmental and climate advocates. Despite an avowed commitment to rights-based and "inclusive" approaches to conservation, many global conservation programs continue to violate Indigenous Peoples' land rights and territorial sovereignty. This leads to the third main argument we make in this book. We draw inspiration from the collective articulation and intimate engagements between Indigenous Peoples and their varied environments. Yet, transforming global environmentalism would require building broad-based coalitions among rural and urban communities, including residents of global metros. This is where transnational youth climate movements, such as Fridays for Future and Extinction Rebellion, have an important role to play. In Chapter 6, we track their evolution over the years, discuss their efforts to incorporate key tenets of decolonization in movement demands and strategies, and suggest ways to further deepen these engagements.

We conclude in Chapter 7 by charting new visions of a regenerative and emancipatory decolonial environmentalism. We do this by building on insights from anti-colonial scholars and activists, advocates of Indigenous rights, Black Feminism, and other social movements that have built solidarities and visions for a just and thriving world. Going beyond simply juxtaposing mainstream environmentalism against environmental justice or Indigenous movements, we weave together threads from the ideas, philosophies, and strategies of the select environmental movements in the concluding chapter. This leads us to argue that decolonizing environmentalism is necessary not just for the sake of formerly colonized countries or Indigenous Nations subjected to settler colonialism, but also for imagining a global environmental movement that is just, inclusive, and effective in the long run.

Decolonizing Environmentalism: What Do We Mean? Why Now?

European colonization of the Americas, Africa, Asia, and Oceania established unprecedented patterns of human exploitation and natural resource extraction leading to an unequal world system. Colonialism also thrusted upon the world an influential dualism between society and nature and an accompanying myth that societies can only progress by conquering nature. The continuation of these power differences and nature-society dualism leads to an unfettered extraction of natural resources, such as fossil fuels, minerals, and the exploitation of socially and politically marginalized human communities and non-human species.

The ongoing processes of colonialism have global consequences, including for dominant groups within the Global North. However, discussions of "decolonization" have so far focused mainly on the Global South and Indigenous Nations within the Global North. For a fuller understanding of how the nexus of colonialism and capitalism continues to shape mainstream environmentalism, and to figure out how to decolonize environmentalism, we present a deeper diagnosis. In this chapter, we trace the historical and intellectual roots of the colonization of the environment and the perpetuation of colonial approaches in contemporary capitalism and development cutting across the boundaries between the Global North and the South. As such, decoloniality is not inherently anti-European or anti-American. Instead, it challenges the presumed universalism of "North Atlantic" ways of thinking and knowing, and to situate Eurocentrism as one of the many strands within a broader intellectual and cultural pluriverse.[1] Decentering of European knowledge would pave the way for bringing diverse perspectives on environmentalism to the proverbial table.

Environmental Racism and Failures of Mainstream Environmentalism

In an 85-mile stretch in Louisiana, between New Orleans and Baton Rouge, lies America's "Cancer Alley," which is home to seven of the ten census tracts with the highest incidence of cancer in the United States.[2] This includes Freetown, established in 1872 by freed African Americans, in St. James Parish. They sought to make a fresh start, to live in peace, hoping for better lives for their children, hopes that the civil rights movement bolstered further. Yet, over the decades, residents of Cancer Alley have been subjected to unacceptably high levels of toxicants in air and water. Fossil fuel corporations run more than 150 toxic facilities here and are responsible for perpetrating environmental racism, and in the words of some residents, a form of genocide.[3]

Another 170 miles to the west, in the Lake Charles area, a similar toxic industrial complex run by South African Synthetic Oil Limited (SASOL) sickens the majority Black population of the area.[4] SASOL's legacy of environmental racism cuts across international borders and time. Established by South Africa's apartheid government, SASOL adopted and perfected a technique invented by the Nazis during the Second World War to create liquid fuel by mixing natural gas and coal. During apartheid, SASOL reinforced racial privileges through exclusive employment of white workers. In post-Apartheid South Africa, SASOL's employees are more diverse, but its operations have created a "Cancer Valley" between central Durban and Durban harbor, affecting a primarily Black population of 100,000.[5] Half the school kids here have asthma, and leukemia is twenty-four times more likely than in other parts of the country.

From Cancer Alley to Cancer Valley, the "empire always strikes back" no matter how far the oppressed flee.[6] These are just two examples of the widely pervasive phenomenon of "environmental racism," working within the interstices of capitalism and Western liberal democracies. Civil rights leader Rev. Benjamin Chavis defined environmental racism as a form of structural racism that works through the "enforcement of regulations and laws, the deliberate targeting of communities of color for siting of toxic waste facilities, the official sanctioning of life-threatening presence of poisons and pollutants in our communities, and the history of excluding people of color from leadership of environmental movements."[7]

Despite racial minorities and the poor routinely bearing unequal costs of fossil fuel and toxic industries, mainstream environmentalism failed to hear their voices. None of the famed environmentalists— including Rachel Carson, Jane Goodall, Erin Brockovich, and others— focused on the racialized effects of environmental pollution. This deafening silence among environmentalists was eventually broken by African American and Latinx communities facing such racism in the United States. EJ scholars have compared the movement to "a river, fed over time by many tributaries."[8] In addition to the Black civil rights movement, which inspired the 1982 EJ protests in Warren County, North Carolina, other streams of EJ movement owe their origins to the Latinx farmworkers' unions and movements in California.[9]

The EJ movement successfully brought environmental racism and inequalities to the center of policy debates and on the radar for a section of the environmental community. Yet, the conceptualization of the environmental justice movement did not account for the histories of settler colonialism and its effects on Indigenous Nations and communities in the United States and beyond. The conjoined histories of colonialism and capitalism have contributed to the large-scale dispossessions of Indigenous Peoples and decimation of their ecological life-support systems in North America and other parts of the world.[10] Despite the shared experiences of marginalization and environmental racism experienced by Black, Indigenous, economically poor, and other communities of color, each of these groups is embedded in particular historical processes and face very different political and institutional constraints.

Indigenous scholar-activist Dina Gilio-Whitaker argues that for Indigenous Nations in the United States, rectifying environmental injustices is not just a question of fair distribution of access to environmental amenities. To her, Indigenous environmental justice requires fixing the long-lasting and continuing effects of settler colonialism by recognizing Indigenous sovereignty and returning Indigenous lands to their rightful stewards.[11] The US government agencies, especially the US Army Corps of Engineers, US Navy, and other security agencies, have been implicated in numerous violations of Indigenous territorial sovereignty. The Navajo Nation and other Indigenous Nations have suffered the long-lasting consequences of the development and testing of nuclear warheads. The efforts to clean up the sites contaminated by nuclear waste led environmental experts in the United States to coin the euphemism "sacrifice zone," which describes areas that were "damaged irreparably" by testing and manufacturing of nuclear weapons, and which became "inhospitable to life—humans, animals, plants."[12] The phenomenon of sacrifice zones aptly describes the violence of modern development, including the effects of mining, industrial development, and mega dams meant to produce "renewable" hydropower.

This brings us to a basic question: Why has mainstream environmentalism not cared for the racialized effects of environmental destruction? A direct answer could be the lack of diversity in the leadership of the environmental movements. Indeed, mainstream environmentalism continues to be led by members of privileged social groups that have not experienced the brutal impacts of environmental destruction and the toxic remnants of environmental cleanup. Such skewed patterns of leadership in environmental organizations have a strong bearing on the actions and strategies of environmental organizations.[13] However, this is only a partial answer. We argue that representational imbalances within environmentalism are merely one of the symptoms. The root cause lies in the problematic intellectual foundation and colonial histories of mainstream environmentalism. In the following pages, we examine these histories and foundations with the intention of demonstrating their relevance to the goals of decolonizing environmentalism.

Entangled Roots of European Modernity, Colonialism, and Capitalism

Mainstream environmentalism emerged in the colonial era when European elites and colonial administration presented themselves as vanguards of human civilization. While this history is very well documented, it is important to recognize that European colonialism was not an aberration or an unsavory dark spot on the European Enlightenment and modernity. On the contrary, colonialism was a logical result of the way in which European civilization defined itself and its role in remaking world history. For a full understanding of these links, it's helpful to introduce the history of European modernity.

Modernity is often identified with the philosophical, cultural, and scientific changes following the Enlightenment and the scientific revolution in Europe. The ideas and ideology of modernity emerged in the late seventeenth and early eighteenth centuries to contest the primacy of religious worldviews, myths, and traditions.[14] More broadly, emergence and development of modernity occurred at the intersection of ideology, politics, and economy. European

Enlightenment provided the ideological background, and the rise of individualism and the secularization of political power reflected its political dimension. The enclosure of British commons leading to large-scale migration of peasants and farmworkers into cities, commercialization of human labor, and production of commodities for profit-making constituted the economic dimension of modernity.[15] Much of this took place in Europe. Therefore, modernity is presumed to be an exclusively European phenomenon. Yet, historical evidence points to comparable advances in other societies, some of which predated European modernity.

Egyptian elites built the pyramids *c.* 2575 BCE using technologies that were quite "modern." Khufu's pyramid is "the most colossal single building ever erected on the planet," with sides accurately oriented to the four cardinal points of the compass.[16] Similarly, around 2500 BCE, when most Europeans were still not familiar with the plough, a highly advanced and modern Indus Valley Civilization existed in South Asia. It had cities with paved streets and underground sewage systems. A trove of such evidence from other parts of the world points to the existence of "multiple modernities" spread over time and space.[17] Yet, modernity is conflated with Eurocentric notions of intellectual and technological advancements alone.[18] Because of its historical and continuing dominance, we use "European Modernity" and "modernity" interchangeably here and elsewhere in this book. Walter Mignolo has argued that the celebration of modernity, and Western civilization more broadly, also serves to hide its darker side, that is, "coloniality" of European civilization.[19]

European elites thought of colonialism as a mission to civilize the barbarian. The mythical European "self"—a modern, rational subject who had escaped the dark ages of medievalism, especially in the wake of European Enlightenment and European Modernity—was the quintessential opposite of the stereotyped non-European. In the words of Edward Said, one of the most pre-eminent scholars of

Western modernity, " … it can be argued that the major component in European culture is precisely what made that culture hegemonic both in and outside Europe: the idea of European identity as a superior one in comparison with all the non-European peoples and cultures."[20] He goes on to underline the European strategy of a "flexible *positional* superiority, which puts the Westerner in a whole series of possible relationships" with the non-Western societies and peoples "without ever losing him [*sic*] the relative upper hand."[21] From this vantage point, European modernity obfuscates the inherently violent project of European colonization.

Amitav Ghosh's recent historical travelogue, *The Nutmeg's Curse: Parables for a Planet in Crisis,* presents a deeply insightful snapshot of how colonial violence terrorized communities and ruptured the relationship they shared with their environment.[22] The journey that brought nutmeg to European and American homes was paved with unimaginable violence unleashed on the people of the Indonesian archipelago. Similar processes occurred throughout the Global South. Both nature and humans were enslaved and ferried across the seas from Asia, Africa, and Latin America to the new world between the sixteenth and twentieth centuries. Ghosh argues that "when elite Europeans began to see that they could dominate, and indeed exterminate, large numbers of people—that they could move millions of people through enslavement—a mechanistic ideology toward the planet began to arise."[23] This ideology of domination and extractivism went hand in hand with the emergence and expansion of capitalism, which is promoted, ironically, in the name of human choice and freedom.

The foundations of European capitalism were laid by the East India Company (EIC), a monopolistic English company incorporated by royal charter on December 31, 1600. Formed for the exploitation of trade with Southeast and South Asia, the EIC soon took on the role of an agent of British imperialism in India from the early eighteenth century to the mid-nineteenth century.[24] EIC gave birth to European capitalism and loaded it on the backs of brutal exploitation of the labor and resources in the colonies. As Ghosh puts it, "forcibly extracted" labor of Amerindian, African, and other colonized peoples working on farms, factories, mines and plantations gave birth to capitalism in the eighteenth and nineteenth centuries.[25] The exploitation of enslaved labor was not simply an economic phenomenon, though. It was also deeply racialized.

The EIC was also the first corporation to use slave labor at its facilities in Southeast Asia and India as early as the 1620s, not long after twenty enslaved Africans were brought to the British colony of Jamestown, Virginia.[26] As important as these histories are, these historical bonds between racism and capitalism should not be relegated to historical facts. Building on Cedric Robinson's pathbreaking formulation of "Racial Capitalism," Jodi Melamed argues that capitalism "can only accumulate by producing and moving through relations of severe inequality among human groups."[27] In this very specific and unavoidable reliance on inequalities among humans, but also between the powerful humans and non-human living world, capitalism is inherently extractive and is fundamentally imbued with exploitative qualities. Yet, the appeals of capitalism and other Western ideas on environment and development are also a result of longstanding efforts by colonial administrators and thinkers to colonize the hearts and minds of colonial subjects.

Fanon argued that the most insidious effects of colonialism were to make the colonized believe that they were inferior to the colonizer.[28] Kenyan novelist Ngugi wa Thiong'o uses the term "colonial alienation" to describe how this sense of inferiority alienates the colonized from their own culture and language. He sees language to be central to not only culture, but to the entirety of being, including how people imagine themselves in the world, how they relate with each other, how they construct and express their values, how they connect with nature, and how they visualize their destinies.[29] To be clear, imposition of a European way of thinking is inseparable from the exercise of other forms of coercive power through control of material resources in nature and society. Similarly, John Gaventa's classical work shows that the colonial takeover of land and resources in the Appalachian Valley concentrated and reinforced the power of the absentee economic elite to manufacture consent. Patterns of resource control mapped on the "patterns of quiescence and rebellion."[30] This argument also applies to the ways in which most people in the United States demonstrate an unquestioned commitment to a social system designed around consumer capitalism ... [which is] experienced to be simply "the way things are."[31] Indeed, the nexus of Eurocentric approaches to post-colonial development, capitalism, and extractivism is applicable to most parts of the Global South.

Modernity, Progress, and Extractivism

The primary social arrangement in the Western industrial societies works through the forces of consumerism. Most of us cannot imagine our lives without objects such as cars, refrigerators, computers, cell phones, or the internet. These and other scientific and technological advances are "embodiments of modernity's power to diminish distance, forestall the seasons, and render irrelevant the earth's rotation."[32] Yet, all these hallmarks of modernity, including skyscrapers and other urban infrastructure in the cities the world over, are manifestations of large-scale extraction or "inverted mines."[33]

In his 1934 book, *Technics and Civilization*, Lewis Mumford—American philosopher of technology—suggests that verbs such as "mine, blast, dump, crush, extract, exhaust" are "the core syntax of modernity." He also recognizes that "the act of wresting minerals from the earth has historically required the subjugation and

Figure 2 Skyscrapers and energy guzzling billboards in metropolitan cities mask the hazardous labor of the global underclass mining for rare minerals.

Top image: Times Square on June 20, 2022 in New York City. Photo by Noam Galai/Getty Images.
Bottom image: Artisanal miners carry sacks of ore at the Shabara artisanal mine near Kolwezi, Congo, DRC on October 12, 2022. Some 20,000 people work at Shabara, in shifts of 5,000 at a time. Photo by Junior Kannah/AFP /Getty Images.

demeaning of both nature and humankind, as faceless pairs of hands and unseen laboring backs descend into the dark, inhuman hell of tunnels to strip away the organs of nature."[34] In this way, extraction symbolizes the intricate connections between the comforts of the affluent and the drudgery of the laboring classes. Understanding the nexus between development, progress, and extractivism is crucial to a full understanding of the social and ecological consequences of modernity.

Extractivism is a mode of economic development and wealth accumulation that take place through the removal of large quantities of minerals, fossil fuels, and natural resources like farming, forestry, and fishing, which are exported to wealthier countries with little processing.[35] Extractivism is often tied to the goals of production that cater to wealthy consumers with excessive purchasing power. Corporations looking to profit from consumerism have promoted a culture of planned. Some of the most popular consumer products like cellphones, computers, refrigerators, and cars are manufactured to last for a short period of time or lose their functional efficiency and cannot be repaired easily.[36] While there is some regulatory pushback against planned obsolescence favored by big businesses, much needs to be done.[37] The links between modern consumerism and extractivism are forged in political arenas that are intertwined with international and domestic inequalities. Elites within the Global South benefit from and perpetuate the highly unjust and environmentally destructive status quo. Extractivism appears in the guise of anti-colonial arguments about national development in the formerly colonized countries, though the roots of the quest for resource-intensive development trace back to modernity.

Georg Hegel, one of the most influential modern European philosophers, described the trajectory of world history and development as the unstoppable, inevitable movement from immaturity to maturity, from infancy to adulthood. Moreover, Hegel claimed that "the movement of Universal History goes from the East to the West. Europe is the absolute end of Universal History. Asia is its beginning." Hegel was pivotal in establishing what scholars refer to as the "developmental fallacy"—that the world must unilaterally follow the European path of development. For Hegel, to be developed was to be modern in the European sense, and to be non-modern was to be undeveloped. The categories of development and underdevelopment entered economics, sociology, and other disciplines from Hegelian thought.[38] It is worth noting here that modernity is founded on a core belief in endless progress, which economists and policymakers have used to justify the pursuit of perpetual economic growth.[39] The endless pursuit of economic growth is at the heart of extractivist methods that are used to exploit natural resources, and they have directly caused widespread environmental destruction.

The state plays a central role in promoting extractive industries, such as mining, corporate-controlled agri-businesses, or fossil fuels. These industries typically arrive with promises of national and local development, and jobs for the members of local communities or monetary compensations for the displacement and dispossession caused by extractive industries. In some Latin American countries, left and center-left governments have used the income from extractivist development projects to support broad-based social welfare and human development programs.[40] However, in most cases, extractivist projects have led to both environmental degradation and social dislocations. New employment opportunities rarely fill the holes created by lost livelihoods. Extractive industries and governments also fail to provide resources and support needed to compensate for land grabs and environmental harm that result from extractivism.

This plays out at sites for big dams, mining, logging, agribusiness, industrial ranching, commercial plantations, special economic zones, and drilling for oil and gas across the world.[41] And, in the oil and gas pipelines that crisscross Indigenous territories in North America.[42]

Figure 3 Farmers displaced by Omkareshwar dam, standing in water for the last 16 days at Ghogalgaon (Khandwa) demanding decrease in water level of dam and compensation on September 9, 2012 in Ghogalgaon, India.

Photo by Amit Jaiswal/Hindustan Times /Getty Images.

In most cases, neither the products and services, nor the wealth accumulated from extraction benefit those who bear the burdens of extractivism.

This explains why millions—Indigenous Peoples, peasants, and other rural populations—defend their livelihoods, land, and culture by resisting extractivist projects which are almost always presented in the garb of development.[43] Their voices are either drowned out by the cacophony of the promises of progress or they are met with violence. In Chapter 1, we discussed how heroic conservation actions by Euro-American activists are immune to such violence that victimizes environmental defenders like Berta Cáceres. The murders of environmental defenders are often under-reported and their murderers are rarely brought to justice.[44] Such violence is neither an aberration nor incidental, as it is systemically intertwined with extractivist models of development.[45] Equally important, while the violence of extractivism manifests mainly in the Global South, the recent trend of criminalization of environmental dissent in the United States and the UK suggests that the Global North is not immune to it.[46]

Resisting extractivism is important not just for ending human rights violations but also for forging new pathways for development and addressing the root causes of polycrisis.[47] The path to such transformative resistance is pockmarked with confounding effects of resource nationalism and the narratives of economic development, which domestic elites use to disguise vested interests. Equally important, focusing solely on material interests may underestimate the stronghold of Western ideologies of "development" among the middle and upper classes in the Global South. The need to tackle both mind and matter makes it a daunting challenge.

Decolonizing the Mind for Decolonizing Environmentalism

Decolonizing environmentalism requires reimagining the environment and environmental problems beyond the narrow confines of Eurocentrism. The frameworks of coloniality and decoloniality—a South American intellectual movement that began in the 1990s—offer useful insights on how colonialism and neocolonialism shape environmental conservation. Built on foundational work by sixteenth- and seventeenth-century organic intellectuals from Latin America as well as Aime Cesaire, Frantz Fanon, and Edward Said, Decoloniality is a standpoint and practice aimed at "the undoing of Eurocentrism's totalizing claim and frame …."[48] For example, most scientists and social scientists have concluded that our current environmental and climate crisis has their roots in the energy-intensive consumption of a small but affluent section of global population.[49] These imbalances have magnified dramatically in the wake of the unprecedented spike in global and domestic inequalities.[50] Yet, many Western environmentalists routinely place the blame for environmental degradation on overpopulation in the Global South.[51]

Celebrity environmentalists such as David Attenborough, Jane Goodall, and Prince William reproduce neocolonial assumptions and relationships. They promote Western environmental solutions and exclude local communities from their narratives of conservation, as if their missions and campaigns were the only way to save native flora and fauna. Even so, Global North is not immune to the blind spots of mainstream environmentalism. Eurocentric environmentalism also undermines the efficacy of environmental protection efforts in industrially advanced countries. This is evident in the contemporary debates on catastrophic wildfires in the American North-West. While these fires may have been triggered by either natural causes or downed power lines, the root causes of these disasters are tied to the changes in resource stewardship and management practices following the European colonization of the Americas.

The use of carefully supervised low-intensity fire, both as part of Indigenous farming and in Indigenous rituals, helped burn fire-prone undergrowth and reduced overall fire risks. These controlled fires also aided the regeneration of Oak and other native species, and in biodiversity conservation more broadly. The imposition of the Western forestry management practices disrupted Indigenous stewardship of landscapes that they saw as their home. These "scientific" Eurocentric management practices, which the US Forest Service continues to use to date, promote dense growth of brush, which exacerbates the risks of catastrophic wildfires in the face of natural or human-induced triggers. Scientific forestry, which we discuss more in Chapter 4, heightens the risks of catastrophic fires. These effects are magnified by climate change.[52] In some ways, the US Forest Service has acknowledged that it was a mistake to stigmatize and ban Indigenous practices of cultural burn.[53] Yet, similar blind spots continue to shape Western resources management and nature conservation practices that are used widely.

For decolonizing environmentalism, it is imperative to visualize the environment, and environmental problems outside the narrow confines of Eurocentrism. Such a pathway for decolonizing environmentalism requires us to draw upon the knowledge and ingenuity of Indigenous groups, peasant societies, women farmers, nomads, pastoralists, and the urban poor to revive, and in many cases, recreate knowledge that has been bulldozed and buried by the hegemony of modernity, capitalism, and neocolonialism. This decolonized knowledge about the environment can give way to solutions and alternatives that are people-centric and fundamentally anti-colonial. However, the agenda and goals of decolonizing environmentalism cannot be based on a romanticized or essentialized version of Indigenous knowledge fixed in time and space.

Decolonization of knowledge, thinking, methods, and approaches is crucial. Yet, an excessive emphasis on knowledge and its competing interpretations also run the risk of turning this into a metaphor, which is subject to widespread appropriation, as we discuss in the context of sustainability in Chapter 4. To avoid these risks, the goals of decolonization should prompt us to consider difficult questions and, in some cases, hard-to-negotiate trade-offs. Fanon's call for decolonization was based on a type of hybridity that would allow for careful selection and adoption of wisdom from various cultures.[54] Diverse systems of knowledge and praxis can be brought together to create practical ways of addressing problems in ways that respond to the crucial features of local social and environmental context.

By Way of Conclusion: A Framework for Decolonizing Environmentalism

We have argued in this chapter that the movement for decolonization of environmentalism must be based on a careful understanding of the foundational premises of modernity. The notion of "savages" that Europeans associated with Black and Brown people reflected the European beliefs about modernity. Europeans saw themselves as "modern" because they had successfully used science and technology to conquer, tame, and control nature. In this European vision, society could only progress by dominating nature and the environment.[55] The foundations of modernity are rooted in the European colonization of nature as the main marker of being modern. In contrast, European elites looked down on the non-Europeans, who lived a life of savages and died at the mercy of nature.

Using this nature versus civilization binary, Europeans characterized societies outside Europe as pre-modern and used this as a justification to exploit them as a source of raw materials for industries back home. These binaries of nature versus culture and European modernity versus non-European savagery are reflected in the continued dominance of capitalism as an economic system. Scholars of contemporary political economy have shown that the forces of capitalism are inseparable from an imperial dominance of the world economic system. Gurminder Bhambra and Peter Newell argue convincingly that the role of colonialism and imperialism was not just to prepare the ground for capitalism, but the political dominance of Global North is "integral" to the ongoing expansion of capitalism.[56] They argue that "[t]he end of European empires and the rise of new postcolonial nations is not the final realisation of a global, capitalist market economy, but a return to 'colonialism by corporation.'" In this sense, the continued dominance of transnational corporations, especially those profiting from fossil fuels responsible for climate crisis, is not just a matter of balancing the needs of economic development with concerns of environmental and climate change. Regulating capitalism has been difficult precisely because the concentration of wealth drives climate policy obstruction.[57]

Eurocentric prejudices in favor of capitalism also contribute to technocratic and authoritarian tendencies embedded in many of the popular environmental programs and climate solutions.

Decolonizing environmentalism demands dismantling Eurocentric thinking about development, environment, and people. It also requires that international institutions that promote such colonial thinking are held accountable. The interconnectedness of politics, economy, society, and environment is also a reason for environmentalists to support and actively participate in the broader struggles for decolonization and emancipation of the majorities of the world. Decolonizing environmentalism must necessarily include two more elements: one, land reparations; and two, purging environmentalism of the masculine desires of conquering nature.[58] In this critical form, decolonizing environmentalism would primarily be aimed at confronting the settler state's monopoly over the management of land, forests, mountains, grasslands, and non-human species which Indigenous communities regarded as their kin. A decolonized environmentalism of this sort will also be based on a radical rethinking of mainstream environmentalism's vision, philosophy, leadership structures, strategies, and institutions.

Our vision of decolonizing environmentalism is based on the foundational idea that nature and human society are inseparable, which has the potential to radically disrupt the Eurocentrism of mainstream environmentalism. Our imagination of a decolonized environmentalism presumes resistance against the root causes of the ongoing polycrisis—masculine hubris about manipulating the environment; obsession with endless progress, extractivism, violent colonialism, and unfettered profiteering. This is also crucial for confronting environmental racism and to avoid creating more sacrifice zones in the future.[59] Similarly, this respect is contingent on Indigenous sovereignty, and land reparations for Indigenous Nations, everywhere. We also see that an environmentalism of this sort will elicit significant resistance from the powerful defenders of the status quo and society at large, which is implicated in structures of extractivism and a culture of consumerism. These are formidable challenges, but worth fighting for.

Equally important, the Western perspectives on nature and the environment continue to shape dominant strands of environmentalism, such as in proposals for climate geoengineering, which we discuss in the next chapter. A strong push toward these elitist solutions reminds us of a dimension of modernity that is now threatening our future. Modernity is premised on the assumption that humans are both capable of, and *entitled* to, manipulating the universe to serve the goals and aspirations of a small section of humanity.[60] The emerging belief and arrogance about untested technologies of climate geoengineering reflect this attitude. This urge—to play God—detracts from the urgency of scaling down colonial-capitalist systems and their energy-intensive patterns of production and consumption that have pushed us into our contemporary environmental and climate crises. In the next chapter, we explain how the narrative of the Anthropocene and the blinding influence of European Modernity are leading to an increasingly emboldened turn toward highly risky technological solutions to climate crises.

Planet-Hacking Environmentalism in the Anthropocene

Imagine yourself on Virgin Galactic's next space flight. You might fly through layers of sulfur dioxide artificially injected into the stratosphere, reducing the amount of sunlight that reaches the earth's atmosphere. Even if you are on a commercial flight in the near future, you may see fewer cirrus clouds in the sky as they would be thinned out to avoid trapping earth's heat. On an ocean cruise, in a few years, you might encounter a fleet of ships churning out micro bubbles transforming the sea surface into a mirror, reflecting sunlight back toward the sun. You might also see giant fountains spraying sea salt into low-lying clouds, making them shinier than usual and reflecting more sunlight back into space. Even a leisurely drive through the countryside may bring you face to face with high-albedo crops, a fancy name for genetically modified plants with a waxy sheen, engineered to reflect sunlight away from earth's surface.

These futuristic scenes are not dystopian fantasies anymore. Each of these proposals belongs to a class of climate interventions collectively referred to as climate geoengineering (CGE). If a group of scientists, technocrats, and world leaders—most of them from the industrially advanced countries responsible for the climate crisis—have their say, geoengineering will be a reality very soon. The US National Academy of Sciences is hastening the development of these technologies.[1] The specter of geoengineering has prompted us to ask a fundamental question: Why are such outrageous planet-hacking technologies being considered as serious climate solutions? Such scientific and technological adventurism is rooted in European enlightenment and European modernity, which presumes the superiority of technological innovations over precautionary approaches to minimizing environmental degradation. Such myopic emphasis on short-term benefits has pushed us to the brink of environmental and climate catastrophe. Yet, ironically, the same thinking is being applied toward ostensible solutions to the crisis.

Despite the relevance of philosophical debates about modernity and environmentalism, our present crises cannot be attributed to our collective inability to resolve these tedious and somewhat abstract debates. The toolkit of protecting the status quo has other historical precedents, which helps explain the motivations for and the tactics of CGE.

From Climate Denialism to Climate Engineering

Elite appropriation of science often takes place through large corporations and oligarchies. The history of research on cigarettes and their health consequences illustrates the stranglehold that Big Tobacco maintained on science over most of the twentieth century. Cigarette companies sponsored misleading "research," captured the policy process to thwart public health regulations based on genuine scientific research, and launched costly PR campaigns to distract public attention away from scientific research about the near-certain harms of tobacco smoking. Even after independent and publicly funded research on these harms became available, Big Tobacco planted confounding research that they aggressively broadcast.[2] An internal industry memo from 1969 stated, "Doubt is our product."[3] A similar cultivation of doubt about climate change has been in play for decades now.

Though climate denialism is often associated with partisan politics, its roots go back to corporate sponsorship and lobbying, which also influences policymaking on energy and the environment. An IMF report showed that in a sample of 191 countries, fossil fuel subsidies amounted to $7 trillion for the calendar year 2022.[4] This included direct subsidies in the form of incentives and tax waivers worth $1.3 trillion and implicit subsidies, including environmental and health costs, to the tune of $5.7 trillion. Climate denialism is meant to protect these privileges, which would be threatened if governments acted on controlling fossil fuel use for mitigating the root causes of climate change. Beneficiaries of fossil fuel capitalism have therefore invested in muzzling all forms of dissent, including on university campuses. As far back as the 1970s, fossil fuel corporations such as Shell and Exxon Mobil put in place a formidable climate denial machine that denounced climate science and sowed the seeds of confusion among the public. The oil companies, and public relations firms acting on their behalf, recruited contrarian scientists, astroturf front groups, and amateur bloggers, and worked closely with conservative politicians and talk-show hosts.[5]

The long tentacles of climate denialism became evident in the fate of an artwork installed on the University of Wyoming campus in 2012. This installation, entitled "Carbon Sink: What Goes Around Comes Around," designed by British landscape artist Chris Drury, had a 36-foot-wide circle of logs from beetle-infested trees, arranged in a whirlpool pattern around a pile of coal. It was meant to trigger conversations about dead forests and anthropogenic climate change. In May 2012, just after students left campus for the summer, the artwork disappeared. An investigative journalist reported that after the installation, Marion Loomis, president of the Wyoming Mining Association, had written to the university asking: "What kind of crap is this?"[6] Both industry representatives and state legislators weighed in on the artwork, some threatening the university's funding, eventually forcing university administration to cave in. Fortunately, climate denialism is not winning.

Despite the political and economic power of the fossil fuel industry, climate denialism has been confronted with growing consensus around climate science, which shows that we are already in the middle of a climate catastrophe. Climate movements, especially those led by young activists, have brought awareness of the climate crisis to the majority of people in the Global North. Anticipating these changes, perpetrators of climate change have switched from climate denialism to delay tactics. Most of these actors now accept the reality of climate change but emphasize short-term negative economic effects of climate policies, including the apparently prohibitive costs of climate mitigation.[7] More interestingly, the failure to undertake timely and effective climate mitigation, caused largely by climate denialism, is now being weaponized for using reckless technologies of Solar Geo-Engineering (SGE). "As Humans Fumble Climate Challenge, Interest Grows in Geoengineering," reads the title of an opinion piece published in *Forbes* magazine.[8]

SGE is a subset of new planetary adventures collectively called Climate Geo-engineering (CGE). It includes technologies designed to deliberately alter the Earth's climatic system, in an attempt to limit the adverse impacts of global climate change. A second type of climate geoengineering, called carbon dioxide removal (CDR), is designed to remove large quantities of carbon dioxide from the atmosphere. One prominent form of CDR, called bioenergy with carbon capture and storage (BECCS), seeks to capture atmospheric carbon by planting bioenergy crops over an area almost twice the size of India, then burning the bio-crops to generate power in thermal power plants, capturing the carbon released in the process, and finally injecting the captured carbon deep inside the earth's core.[9] Such high-tech plans make the fantastic title of Clive Hamilton's book actually sound realistic—*Earth Masters: Playing God with the Climate.*

It is crucial to take a step back from these adrenaline-producing Sci-Fi interventions and ask if these interventions will tackle the root causes of the crisis? They do not. SGE, for example, does nothing about problems caused by increased concentration of atmospheric carbon such as extreme air pollution and acidification of the oceans from the absorption of atmospheric carbon in the oceans. On the other hand, by altering atmospheric temperature, SGE could potentially cause massive disruptions in the global hydrological cycle.[10] The implications of climate geoengineering for summer monsoons, crucial for the lives and livelihoods of at least 2 billion people in Asia and Africa, should be a good enough reason to halt SGE development.[11] Similarly, large-scale rapid land use change required for growing bioenergy crops under BECCS cannot happen without trampling over land, forest, and water rights of millions of people who subsist on these resources. It is also very likely to further strain already precarious global food security, perhaps many times more serious than the 2008 food crisis, which a World Bank report attributed to the sudden increase in the area of land planted with biofuel crops. The effects of these land use changes continued to be felt nearly a decade after the 2008 spike in global food prices.[12]

Going by the tenets of the precautionary principle, CGE should be understood as an unprecedented adventure that risks planetary health. It entails polluting the atmosphere with sunlight-reflecting aerosols or large-scale burning of bioresources for the narrow goal of bringing down average global atmospheric temperature (in the case of SGE) or carbon capture (in the case of CDR). Yet, there is a growing number of environmentalists, climate engineers, social scientists, and even progressive activists who advocate the use of CGE solutions. This includes the leftist periodical *Jacobin* that paints geoengineering as part of "a comprehensive vision of ecological reconstruction."[13]

Predictions about the effects of geoengineering interventions, especially the SGE, are based entirely on climate modeling and forecasting, with very large uncertainties. Climate scientists acknowledge that there are several known and unknown unknowns in the science of atmospheric dynamics.[14] Computer models tell us little about the changes that the introduction of new chemicals in the stratosphere could trigger or the potential geological responses to large-scale pumping of solidified carbon deep into the earth's core. Why then are some scientists, their powerful supporters in governments, global philanthropies, and even some activists ready to risk the planet for the sake of these unpredictable adventures?

While ongoing efforts to understand risks and benefits of CGE technologies are necessary, it is clear that science alone cannot show us the path forward. Social scientists argue that the wisdom of researching geoengineering, as one component of a climate policy portfolio, must be debated vigorously, through the development of international SGE governance lest we unleash irreversible harms.[15] Others argue that such climate "solutions" developed in elite circles are not even based on scientific knowledge about climate change or climate mitigating actions. Instead, these scholars characterize these solutions as knee jerk reactions catalyzed by fear and uncertainty of a global elite invested in maintaining their privileges.[16] An international group of academics, including climate scientists and renowned writers, has demanded a global moratorium on the development of SGE.[17]

All these efforts notwithstanding, we must ask why despite untested promises and unforeseen risks, these technologies are being pursued so fervently? We believe there are two types of explanations for the aggressive advocacy of SGE. First, SGE advocates tend to be "primarily white men at elite institutions in the Global North, funded largely by billionaires, corporations, or their philanthropic arms."[18] In this sense, there is strong resonance with findings about the support for climate denialism, which was strongest among conservative white men motivated by the goals of protecting their advantage within the status quo.[19] A second, and more profound reason goes back to the long shadow of

European Modernity, which socialized majority of people in the North Atlantic world to believe in the promise of science and technology to solve the planetary crisis. This technological hubris anchored in the European Enlightenment continues to shape modern science and mainstream thinking about climate crises. The Promethean tendencies of Eurocentric science have potentially dangerous consequences for a planet battered by multiple social, environmental, and climate crises. We conclude this chapter by investigating the broader reverberations of Eurocentrism and European modernity in debates surrounding the Anthropocene.

Figure 4 Åsa Larsson Blind, the vice president of Saami Council, an Indigenous People's Organization that successfully stopped a Harvard University experiment to conduct test flights for research and development of solar geoengineering technology at the Swedish Space Corporation based in Sápmi in their homeland. The Saami Council spoke out against the experiment, objecting to the lack of consultation about research conducted on and above their homeland and any solar geoengineering development, regardless of where it took place.

Photo by Linnea Nordström/Arctic Council Secretariat/Flickr cc

The Anthropocene: Valorizing the Failures of Modernity?

The Anthropocene is the new bandwagon in the environmental community, though different groups use the idea in different ways, at times with contradictory implications. Global environmental changes prompted several geologists to argue that Earth may have entered a new human-dominated epoch called the Anthropocene.[20] It is defined in the popular press as "the most recent period in Earth's history when human activity started to have a significant impact on the planet's climate and ecosystems."[21] The term was popularized in 2000 by Atmospheric Chemist Paul J Crutzen, along with Biologist Eugene Stoermer. Crutzen, a Nobel laureate who passed away in January 2021, was also an influential advocate of solar geoengineering that we discussed above. After much debate, the International Union of Geological Sciences (IUGS) rejected the Anthropocene proposal in March 2024. The IUGS argued that the proposal for marking the beginning of the Anthropocene in 1952 failed to account for the deeper history and the ultimate causes of planetary crisis currently underway.[22]

Despite this major setback, the Anthropocene appears as a radical understanding of where we are in our battle to save the planet. It is quite popular in mainstream and social media, popular culture, sciences, social sciences, and humanities, and appears regularly in literary creations. While this new terminology could have triggered a rethink of fundamental meanings of progress and development, Anthropocene is now being deployed as a legitimizing device for technocratic and potentially authoritarian approaches to deal with environmental crises. At a workshop held in November 2019, a geologist declared without any qualms that geologists alone have the expertise to lead planetary stewardship in the Anthropocene.[23] The totalizing sentiments expressed by this geologist are widely shared among influential scientists and policymakers and popularized by the electronic media, philanthropists like Bill Gates, and influential forums, such as the World Economic Forum.[24]

While some promoters of the Anthropocene are careful to refer to it as the "Age of Humans," many, including the National Geographic Society, use "Age of Man." We find this christening deeply problematic. While the phrase "Age of Man" is symptomatic of a machoistic domination of planet Earth, Age of Humans, shields colonialism, capitalism, and the tiny minority—the most affluent 1 percent—largely responsible for damaging the planet. Deflecting the blame on humanity, most of whom have played no role in creating contemporary environmental crises, is disingenuous at best. Scientists, academics, and many climate activists concerned about the fate of humanity's future tend to reify the Anthropocene, while ignoring the long history of capitalism and colonialism that are the main reasons for the onset of this epoch.

A number of critical scholars have cautioned against the simplistic adoption of this approach. In 2014, a group of anthropologists collectively proposed the term "Plantationocene" for the radical transformation of traditional farms, pastures, and forests into industrial plantations, which draws attention to "the historical relocations of the substances of living and dying around the Earth as a necessary prerequisite to their extraction."[25] Yet, the proponents of Plantationocene have been critiqued for conceptualizing plantations "as a system of human control over nature, obscuring the centrality of racial politics," which formed the core of the plantation system.[26]

A number of other scholars converge on the alternative name "Capitalocene," or the age of capital.[27] We build on insights from these scholars to critique two assumptions of the Anthropocene, and use this discussion to advance debates on decolonizing environmentalism. First, we argue that the Anthropocene reinforces the artificial nature-society distinction rooted in European modernity. Second, and even more importantly, the popular understanding of the concept of the

Anthropocene celebrates rather than contests or rejects extractive modernity, which has pushed us into the multiple social, cultural, and environmental crises that we find ourselves in.

Andrew Revkin, a Guggenheim Fellow and noted journalist, wrote the following poem about humanity's influence on earth systems:

> Humanity is etching its signature across its
> Earthscape: diverting waterways, extracting essentials,
> transforming the air, scratching pathways.
> The advance is as inexorable, and natural,
> as that of rust on iron or microbes on a plate of agar.
> We till that which can be tilled, and therefore must
> be tilled, until our outward press meets
> sterile soils. But as we gain a global view,
> and regard our transformed sphere, we
> now ponder an unavoidable question: What next?[28]

For Revkin, the nearly irreversible environmental impacts that mark the Anthropocene are unavoidable costs of the pursuit of progress. This narrative of "calculus of progress" is rooted in Eurocentrism.[29] Such an endless "progress" *necessarily* entails environmentally destructive extractivism, which leads to exploitation of fellow humans and extinction of non-human species. A universally shared march of progress is not responsible for overexploitation and overconsumption of natural resources, degradation of earth's regenerative capacities, and environmental crises. Yet, these devastating consequences are often dismissed amidst uncritical celebrations of European modernity and economic growth. This is also evident in the debates on societal responses to the climate crisis.

The Global North is increasingly recognizing the need to transition away from fossil fuel-driven economies. This has unleashed very high social demand for renewable energy infrastructure, including wind turbines, solar panels, and electric vehicles. This demand, however, remains intertwined with neocolonial tendencies to claim righteous stakes in Lithium and other rare minerals. A *Washington Post* editorial on Chile's Constitutional referendum of September 2022 started as follows: "Lithium is a key input in batteries that run millions of laptops and upon which the United States is basing its electrified automotive future. Chile sits atop the world's largest lithium reserves ... That's reason enough to pay attention to Chile's impending Sept. 4 referendum on a proposed new constitution."[30] This editorial is symptomatic of a new scramble for rare minerals, fueled by the insatiable demands of a rapidly developing renewable energy infrastructure. In seeing the democratic rights of Chileans through the prism of US demand for Lithium, the *Washington Post* editors revealed their discomfort with the imminent constitutional reforms, which would have strengthened the voices of Indigenous Peoples and other marginalized groups in how Chile's mineral wealth should be managed.

The social and environmental consequences of this large-scale "transition" to renewables, which some commentators refer to as "Green Delusion"—raise the specter of "Fossil Fuel+."[31] These mammoth-sized renewable energy grids are new avatars of extractive global capitalism. Without a concerted effort to reduce energy-intensive consumption, the renewable energy transition will continue to follow capitalism's destructive obsession with extraction and commodification. Climate change turns into yet another opportunity for accumulating profits, as can be seen in the hype around carbon offsets and renewable energy derivatives. These Green Delusions are already perpetuating neocolonialism, predatory capitalism, and are on track to further the concentration of wealth and power among elites, dispossession of the poor, more dangerous forms of extractivism, and furthering the destruction of the planet.[32]

Geographers Joel Wainwright and Geoff Mann have outlined the emergence of a planetary regime of control and regulation—a Climate Leviathan—intended to protect the status quo of highly concentrated wealth and vulgar inequalities. Early signs of a capitalist Climate Leviathan can already be seen in the way global climate policy is dominated by technological and market-based solutions, which concentrate the benefits of climate action in corporations in the Global North. Thousands of fossil fuel lobbyists swarm annual meetings of the UN Framework Convention on Climate Change (UNFCCC).[33] Wainwright and Mann see the emergent Climate Leviathan capable of "panopticon-like capacity to monitor the vital granular elements of our emerging world: fresh water, carbon emissions, climate refugees, and so on."[34]

Such planetary regimes of power and control have been dreamt and described not just by the likes of Genghis Khan, Alexander the Great, or Adolf Hitler but also by scientific and political elites. Wainwright and Mann remind us of one such contemporary figure, John Holdren, a Harvard physicist who was a senior advisor in the Obama administration. Holdren co-authored a textbook in 1977 that described such a regime:

> Perhaps those agencies, combined with [the United Nations Environment Programme] and the United Nations population agencies, might eventually be developed into a Planetary Regime— sort of an international superagency for population, resources, and environment. Such a comprehensive Planetary Regime could control the development, administration, conservation, and distribution of all natural resources ... The Regime might also be a logical central agency for regulating all international trade, perhaps including assistance from [developed countries] to [less developed countries], and including all food on the international market. The Planetary Regime might be given responsibility for determining the optimum population for the world and for each region and for arbitrating various countries' shares within their regional limits. Control of population size might remain the responsibility of each government, but the Regime would have some power to enforce the agreed limits.[35]

Holden's proposal should be considered a helpful reference, especially as the debates on population control are seeing a revival.[36] A group of scientists recently issued a global appeal for women and men to have at most one child, arguing that "stabilizing and ultimately reducing the human population size is necessary to ensure the long-term wellbeing of our species and other life on Earth."[37] Indeed, the revival of interest in population growth is prompted by competing arguments by another set of scientists who have issued a "scientists' warning on affluence," arguing that "affluent citizens of the world are responsible for most environmental impacts ... transition towards sustainability can only be effective if far-reaching lifestyle changes complement technological advancements."[38]

Clearly, even as the world stares at the risks of the development of planet-hacking technologies, the debates on environmental and climate crises will continue to unfold on many different planes. These debates provide opportunities for a fresh look at popular ideas such as sustainability, especially influential among college-educated and younger global citizens. In the next chapter, we trace the history of sustainability, the reasons for its adoption by corporations, and its implications for consumerism and extractivism.

Seductions of Sustainability in Contemporary Environmentalism

Aspirations for sustainable living are shared widely. Many of us begin our day by paying homage to it through a compostable K-Cup or by stepping into our favorite independent café for a cup of responsibly harvested coffee. The most popular definition that informs these sustainability strategies appeared in the 1987 report of the Brundtland Commission: "Sustainable development is development that meets the needs of the present without compromising the ability of future generations to meet their own needs."[1] This definition is so broad that it speaks to a wide range of concerns among actors in society, markets, and states. This is why scholars define this as a boundary term to help connect different domains of knowledges and practices. The broadness of the terms sustainability and sustainable development allows people to interpret it differently, spawning a large number of ideas and approaches to sustainable living. Youth activists see sustainable development as a means for pursuing multiple goals of environment, development, and social justice. However, the popularity of sustainability and sustainable development masks the challenges of operationalizing it, and the ambiguities of its implications for various social, economic, and environmental concerns.

To unpack the complexities of sustainability and sustainable development, we trace the concept's origins in concerns much older than the often-cited Brundtland Commission report. The roots of "sustainability" trace back to forest management by European colonial agencies, which offers an additional explanation of why sustainability has not translated into significant environmental protections. We then examine how some of the most popular "tools" of sustainability shape our engagement with issues of environmental stewardship. In conclusion, we reflect on the admirable attempts at infusing sustainability with the ideals of justice.

Sustainability: The Colonial History of a Seemingly Benevolent Idea

It may come as a disappointment to many sustainability advocates that the roots of sustainability go back to colonial exploitation of forests and other natural resources in the early eighteenth century. The term was first used in German forestry circles by Hans Carl von Carlowitz's *Sylvicultura Oeconomica* published in 1713.[2] By sustainable use of forest resources, Carlowitz meant maintaining a balance between harvesting of old trees and growing new trees to replace the harvested stands.[3] This may sound harmless, even desirable—who doesn't like to plant more trees? But in practice, the "old trees" means old growth forests containing a diverse mix of native trees and underbrush that sustained rich ecosystems.

Commercial forestry replaces old growth forests and diverse ecosystems, which serve many human and non-human communities, with monocrops of fast-growing tree species. Thus "sustainable use" of forests transforms rich forest ecosystems into ecologically impoverished but commercially attractive tree crops. Rural communities, peasants, and Indigenous groups often depend on forests, pastures, forest produce, and natural landscapes that are crucial to their livelihoods and cultures. Impoverished ecosystems cause impoverishment of people. The sustainable forestry of the colonial era reproduced such effects in all colonized lands. For example, Dietrich Brandis, a world-renowned German forester, who had established a Forest Service for the colonial government of British India, also played a key role in the founding of US Forest Service. Brandis became Gifford Pinchot's mentor and teacher, using highly detailed hand-written letters to lay out the structure and functions of a federal forestry organization, which provided the blueprint Pinchot used to create the US Forest Service.[4] Because of the special significance of colonial forestry in India from mid-nineteenth century onward, it is instructive to discuss the effects there on forest people and forestlands.

Sustained supplies of timber were essential for building cargo ships for the Royal Navy, which was the central force charged with the expansion and maintenance of the British empire. Meeting the colonial demands for timber in a predictable manner necessitated accurate estimates of "sustainable yields" from forests in India, Burma, Malaysia, and other British colonies. The impacts of colonial forestry on forests and forest-dependent people of the colonies were quite profound and persist even today. The colonial administrations in India, and elsewhere, upended customary rights of people over forests to secure state ownership and control of forests and forestlands. This large-scale legal dispossession transformed forest-dependent people into "illegal occupants" of their ancestral lands.

Unlike Indigenous Americans dispossessed by European colonizers who were offered a semblance of agency, even if as a pretense, those dispossessed by British colonial forestry regimes were neither consulted nor asked for consent through treaties. Instead of setting aside minimum land for the exclusive use of Indigenous Peoples, the forest administration goaded the dispossessed to live in mobile forest settlements that functioned as labor camps for colonial logging operations. To compensate for their labor, colonial forestry officials allowed these communities to grow subsistence crops within commercial tree crops. These communities, however, were expected to be available for working in forestry operations at all times and without much of an advanced notice.[5] Environmental historians have compared this practice to corvée labor.[6] In essence, life for Indigenous victims of sustainable forestry turned hellish.

The longest-lasting and the most profound impact of colonial pursuit of sustainable forestry has been in the form of land dispossession and natural resource conflicts. Worldwide, the so-called "sustainable forest management systems" put in place by colonial governments, and continued by successive post-colonial governments, have victimized an estimated 400 million to 1.5 billion people.[7]

The legacy of the colonial models of forestry and natural resource management continues to shape contemporary debates on the links between the environment and economic development, which is often erroneously equated with energy-intensive and extractive models of economic development. In this section, we highlight select evidence against this simplistic trade-off. Such a narrow understanding of "development" fails to account for important aspects of human development, care economy, and ecofriendly models of agriculture and resource management that contribute to environmental conservation. There is ample evidence about the potential of community-forestry and other community-based experiments that help address the goals of social justice and environmental protection.[8] Yet, such experiments have rarely been replicated on a larger-scale because nearly 85 percent of the global forest area is owned by national forestry agencies deeply invested in the status quo. Evidence from siting of nature-protected

> "Heaven is miles and miles of forest and
> glade without any forest guards."
>
> —A member of the Gond tribe from central India.

Figure 5 An Indigenous imagination of heaven from central India.[9]

areas in a global sample of 137 countries shows that a combination of domestic economic inequalities and weak democratic institutions helps explain the proliferation of exclusionary models of environmental conservation interventions.[10] Recent research provides renewed support for these findings, showing that new global forest restoration plans reinforce past inequalities; agricultural lands in the poorest countries, without effective democratic institutions, are the main targets for global restoration priority maps.[11]

Ironically, recent research shows that "scientific forestry," with its roots in colonial agendas, is neither very scientific nor responsive to local ecological contexts.[12] Neither colonial administrations nor their post-independence successors conducted new research about native tree species that were part of old growth forests. Instead, they "mastered" the assembly line science of developing and growing commercially valuable, yet ecologically impoverished, fast-growing tree monocrops. These widely known failures notwithstanding, forestry agencies are rarely held accountable because they often attract sizable multilateral and bilateral grants and subsidized loans aimed at promoting commercially attractive sustainable forest management or exclusionary wildlife and biodiversity conservation programs. Governments routinely prioritize such funding over investing in scientific research or people-centric policies.

The material and ideological support that international conservation groups provide creates perverse incentives that motivate government agencies to shun transparency, refuse accountability, and create organizational cultures that hinder sound research and innovation.[13]

Big conservation NGOs partner with corporations whose business operations cause large-scale destruction of ecosystems, such as palm oil companies responsible for decimating peat moss forests in Southeast Asia. Multilateral research organizations, such as the Center for International Forestry Research (CIFOR), have worked "assiduously" to develop protocols for the oxymoronic goal of sustainable palm oil production yet have done little research to understand the Indigenous science of forest and ecosystem management.[14] In most cases, commercial pressures linked to large-scale palm oil, timber, ranching, and plantation industries lead to forest degradation. Yet, poor communities become easy targets of prejudices that big conservation NGOs imply and disseminate insidiously. As we show in Chapter 5, the colonial nature of contemporary international conservation is intertwined closely with the expansion of capitalistic appropriation of the ecosystems, landscapes, and natural resources that are the lifelines of rural and Indigenous communities.[15] Overall, global projects of sustainable forest management, nature conservation, and "sustainable development" have failed to stem commercial exploitation of natural resources, while continuing to target new lands used traditionally by rural and Indigenous communities in the Global South.[16]

The Social and Political Costs of Sustainable Development

The most important global statement on sustainable development (SD) is found in the Rio Declaration of 1992. Yet, the declaration turned out to be so ineffective in practice that by the time of Rio+20 conference in 2012, many in the global environmental policy community wanted to forget it.[17] Despite such failures, SD has gained prominence in the feel-good, jargon-filled world of global diplomacy.

One of the most frequently cited articles from the Rio Declaration is Agenda 21, which focuses on promoting public participation for developing and enforcing SD. While it is an important statement of intent, in practice it has remained a symbolic gesture. Poor communities and their interests have remained marginal to global environmental negotiations. These failures notwithstanding, SD has become a rallying cry for environmentalists, especially in the Global North. In 2015, it was institutionalized in global forums in the form of UN Sustainable Development Goals (SDGs) for 2030. As a result, SD has very important policy implications and a great deal of political significance. A part of this significance is rooted in how the ambiguities inherent in SD allow repackaging of the deeply entrenched inequalities between the interests of the market, state, and society under the status quo. Consider the following blurb from the UN sustainable development portal:

> The 2030 Agenda for Sustainable Development, adopted by all United Nations Member States in 2015, provides a shared blueprint for peace and prosperity for people and the planet, now and into the future. At its heart are the 17 Sustainable Development Goals (SDGs), which are an urgent call for action by all countries— developed and developing—in a global partnership. They recognize that ending poverty and other deprivations must go hand-in-hand with strategies that improve health and education, reduce inequality, and spur economic growth—all while tackling climate change and working to preserve our oceans and forests. [18]

This blurb and the accompanying web portals promise all the good things one can imagine neatly wrapped in colorful SDG logos. It also suggests that governments are investing significantly in the programs and policies aimed at achieving SDGs. However, in most cases governments have invested very little in pursuing such a large-scale program aimed at addressing social deprivations and socioecological impacts of extractive development (more on this in Chapter 5). Instead, both governments and the UN are looking up to the business sector to help achieve SDGs. This lends legitimacy to the corporate efforts to use SDGs as public relations tools to promote their business interests. As Claus Stig Pedersen, Head of Corporate Sustainability & Public Affairs, at the Danish corporation

Novozymes says, "The UN Sustainable Development Goals are a Great Gift to Business!"[19]

In some cases, businesses have exploited the narratives of sustainability to coin concepts such as "sustainable consumer demand," where "sustainable" simply means continuing to fuel consumer demand in perpetuity. In most cases, the effects of "sustainable consumer demand" would undermine the goals of environmental or ecological sustainability. The impact of market-friendly sustainability initiatives reverberates far beyond the localities that are riddled with non-biodegradable waste. Those impacts are related to the upstream processes of mining and extraction of natural resources, often under deplorable working conditions.

The production and circulation of "sustainable" commodities connect human communities from different parts of the globe into asymmetric relationships. For example, solar panels, windmills, and batteries for electric vehicles require minerals, such as cobalt, copper, and nickel, which are mined under exploitative labor conditions, without robust environmental regulations.[20] Sure, some climate scholars and activists have begun to discuss ways of moderating the demand for rare minerals.[21] However, the sales of sports utility vehicles (SUVs) have been growing at an unprecedented rate in both Europe and the United States.[22] Unfortunately, electric car makers in the United States are also prioritizing large and crossover models (called EUVs) over smaller electric cars.[23]

Mining of rare minerals is also associated with increased demands for groundwater which undermines local social and ecological systems.[24] More importantly, a rapid increase in renewable infrastructure in the Global South may contribute simultaneously to climate resilience of some sections of society, while making mine workers and nearby communities even more vulnerable. It is virtually impossible to separate concerns for sustainability from the multiple, competing visions of development. Yet, these challenges are often ignored by the urge to use "sustainability" as a catch-all solution for environmental crises.

For a full appreciation of these complex relationships, it is helpful to review three radically different visions of development. The first and the most popular meaning of development is economic development which is identified with economic growth, rising GDP, comforts, and indulgences such as SUVs and other avenues of luxury consumption. The second meaning of development pertains to human development, which emphasizes the provision of amenities such as affordable healthcare, sanitation, education, and meaningful employment. Human development is often identified as "a process of enlarging people's choices ... and strengthening human capabilities" so that they lead longer, healthier, and fuller lives.[25] The third meaning of development is tied to social and political agency of individuals, such that they have the freedom and abilities to set their own development priorities and goals, rather than participate in developmental agendas set by others.

The most popular notions of development, associated with prosperity, and luxurious lifestyles—think superyachts, chartered private planes, and luxury bunkers—are not sustainable anymore because of their vast environmental impact. This form of development is also socially unviable, as evident from the extreme income and wealth inequalities that have grown rapidly over the recent decades.[26] Yet, in practice, economic development cannot be substituted entirely by human development. Some types of economic investments are needed to secure basic amenities such as safe drinking water, sanitation, decent road networks, and public transportation.

Development economists such as Mahbub ul Haque, Amartya Sen, and Martha Nussbaum proposed the concept of "human development" to broaden the focus of development beyond statistics, such as gross domestic product and economic growth. Human development offers an alternative perspective on development that is useful not just for the so-called "third world" but all societies.[27] However, instead of seeing this as a holistic notion of development, those vested in unsustainable luxury-oriented development disparage "human development" as the need for the Global South alone. Such is the stigma of backwardness associated with "human development" that the US government has yet to publish a national human development report.[28] This attitude is shocking considering the widespread human development deprivations within the United States.

An estimated 43 million or 21 percent of US adults do not possess English literacy skills required to compare and contrast information, paraphrase, or make basic inferences.[29] The US Census Bureau reports that in 2018, 11.8 percent of the country's population lived in poverty. Incredible as it may sound, these numbers do not tell the whole story about the nature of development deficits in some parts of the United States. Environmental and social justice activist Catherine Flowers brought to light the fact that many communities of color still live in hookworm-infested environments, a condition often associated with the poorest countries on the planet.[30]

Despite the broader focus of human development, some argue that it simplifies complex dimensions of development into reductive indicators. Moreover, a country's economic growth is built into the formula for computation of human development index, which assumes that greater GDP growth promotes greater human development. However, this is clearly not supported by evidence. For instance, despite growth in aggregate national income, some sections of the US population have experienced a declining wellbeing, giving rise to a "negative trickle down" effect, while supporting profligate consumption among the wealthiest.[31] Indeed, rising global inequalities point to similar problems in most advanced economies. These outcomes are not a coincidence or outcomes of badly designed policies that can be fixed easily. Instead, these outcomes reflect a commitment to economic policies that are designed to serve the interests of the powerful. A growing number of academics and activists argue that it is time to reject the faulty assumptions that lionize "economic growth" as a sign of social progress. Instead, they are calling for "degrowth."

Proposals for degrowth present a radical challenge against mainstream notions of economic growth. They advocate "an ensemble of environmental and redistributive policies," including universal basic minimum income, reduction of working hours, environmental and consumption taxes, and significant regulations on advertising.[32] Instead of being an economic or public policy proposal, degrowth asks for a fundamental shift in cultural, political, and economic imaginaries.[33] In a nutshell, degrowth values social well-being more than it does GDP or economic growth, an ideal that a country like Iceland is sincerely engaging with.[34] Degrowth calls for democratically led lowering of social metabolism—the exchange of materials and energy between physical and biological systems—and moving beyond market-based relations as the sole mechanism of exchange.[35] Degrowth builds on an impressive array of local initiatives across the globe such as solidarity-based exchanges, local currency systems, agroecological models of food sovereignty, co-housing projects, pedestrian- and cyclist-friendly infrastructure, energy cooperatives, decentralized solar power, and meaningful employment.[36]

Degrowth has attracted the attention of decolonial feminist scholars, who argue that the concept of care can reset the growth imaginary and bring about radical change. Their vision contributes to the degrowth vision of building societies "based on caring relations, wellbeing, and equity …"[37] Departing from liberal feminism popular in the Global North, these scholars bring an intersectional lens that accounts for gender, race, class, ethnicity, sexuality, religion, and colonial positionality to bear on the degrowth debate. Equally important, some European degrowth scholars and activists also underline the potential for the degrowth movement to contribute to decolonization. They "call for an end to the colonial patterns of appropriation" and extractivism, which has resulted in industrialized countries accumulating a heavy ecological debt and catastrophic climate breakdown. In this sense, degrowth also speaks to the demands for decolonization.[38] Despite the promises of degrowth and similar proposals for a decolonial future, mainstream environmentalists and sustainability advocates continue to elide these questions. The failure to investigate these structural factors is manifested in what we refer to as the seductions of sustainability.

The Seductions of Sustainability

The true power of boundary concepts, such as sustainability and sustainable development is in their vagueness—they serve as empty signifiers suitable for a multitude of meanings, contexts, and strategies. Few would contest the importance of sustainable tourism or a faith-based group that promises to nurture our souls with spirituality and sustainability. Myriad actors and agencies piggyback on the popularity of these concepts to pursue their own agendas. Corporations utilize it to make their business operations "green," governments use it to justify austerity policies that further emaciate undernourished bodies on earth, and religious leaders deploy it to convince youth that their parents' religion has always cared about the environment.

Sustainability is a marketeer's dream come true because it resonates with a diverse set of potential consumers. Moreover, as we discussed above, there is now a broad international consensus about the importance of pursuing SDGs. Instead of tapping into the narratives of sustainability, we invite you to take the other, more difficult, and more conscientious path—scrutinizing the veracity of claims and evaluating promises within the broader context that shapes policy design, development, and implementation.

Let us begin by reflecting on the cup of joe. Coffee is one of the most ubiquitous items on contemporary menus and has been the subject of various campaigns for sustainability. The demand for coffee has risen greatly over the last fifty years, and it is now coveted in many new places where it was not popular in the past. This should have been good news for coffee farmers but unfortunately, that's not how things have shaped up. The structure of global coffee trade and the network of its long supply chain mean that the laws of demand and supply do not quite work as the introductory economics textbooks would have us believe.

The spike in consumer demand for coffee has led to a race to the bottom where multinational corporations look for ever cheaper sources of coffee. For example, coffee brands often bypass traditional coffee growers in Columbia and Brazil for Vietnam which was virtually unknown in the world of coffee. This brought the price of coffee beans from $3 per pound in the 1970s to 62 cents in the 1990s, driving thousands of Latin American farmers out of business. The price for a pound of Arabica beans at the NY commodities exchange jumped to $2.40 in 2014, then dropped to $1 in the last quarter of 2019, mainly because of a spike in the production of Brazilian coffee. While some consumers pay as much as $6 (sometimes higher in Europe) for a cup of coffee, Burger King and other mass chains have rolled out monthly subscription plans, where one pays $5 a month for two small cups of coffee a day. This dual strategy of low- and high-end coffee consumerism has paid off for coffee retailers, whose net profits have risen manifold. Yet, coffee farmers continue to be paid poorly, which undermines the goals of developing a sustainable coffee supply chain. Underpaid farmers are unlikely to participate in sustainability initiatives under such uncertainty.

There is some evidence to suggest that fair trade coffee continues to "generate real and significant benefits—both material and intangible—for millions of organized small producers across the

Global South. There is more need than ever for *truly* fair trade. The task remains to build a trading system that reflects the movement's founding principles of creating greater economic and social justice in the highly inequitable international commodities trade, and in the global economy generally."[39] On the other hand, other fair trade certificates, such as the Forest Stewardship Council (FSC) Certification of sustainable timber and other forest products, did not invest meaningfully in channeling the benefits of fair trade to smallholders.[40]

Grave concerns remain regarding the complexity of fair trade and organic-labeling markets. The centralization of bodies regulating these certification schemes in industrially advanced countries has led to further marginalization of small-scale producers, especially with the entry of powerful market actors capitalizing on fair trade.[41] A study of Nicaragua's coffee producers shows that over a period of ten years, organic and Fairtrade farmers became poorer relative to conventional producers.[42] A long-term ethnographic study focused on Darjeeling tea plantations, the source of the world's most expensive tea leaves, criticizes fair trade for whitewashing the conditions of servitude under which workers live on plantation estates.[43] Another critic, a fair trade insider, argues that "Fair Trade is a logical continuation of free trade and not a remedy to its weaknesses."[44] The main argument is that the excesses of the market economy cannot be overcome using the same principles and methods. Overall, efforts to promote sustainability without addressing the structural roots of social, economic, and ecological justice are unlikely to achieve the stated goals of fair and ethical trade.

Despite these shortcomings, it is important to understand sustainability as it is perceived and experienced by individual advocates and consumers. A Forest Stewardship Council (FSC) certification makes us happy buying affordable, do-it-yourself Ikea furniture, as we are assured that the furniture was made without destroying invaluable rain forests. It also encourages some to order innumerable packages from amazon.com with smiley logos declaring that the packaging is made of recycled materials. These signs of ostentatious environmentalism have a deep personal importance. To appreciate this, let us take a small detour through psychology 101.

According to Sigmund Freud, "the pleasure principle"—seeking of instinctive pleasure and avoidance of pain—drives much of human impulse. However, social norms regulate our pursuit of such pleasures. So, even when we desire pleasure, a sense of guilt ensures that we forsake pleasure and adhere to norms of socially acceptable behavior. Let us extend Freud's pleasure principle to include consumerism as a means for pleasure and think of environmentally responsible behavior as a relatively new social norm. A true adherence to the social norm favoring environmental care would require most people living in industrially advanced countries to drastically reduce consumption.

However, it is easier to sustain consumption if the products and services we consume are wrapped up in assurances about their sustainable sourcing and supply chain. Declarations such as "FSC certified" and "made from recycled matter" help assuage the guilt associated with unfettered consumption, and thus continue to fuel consumerism.

Slovenian thinker Slavoj Zizek argues that modern capitalism sustains itself by transforming into "cultural capitalism." The cultural dimension of capitalism reimagines the traditional distinction between production and philanthropy into a new schema where consumption and philanthropic morality converge into a unified whole.[45] Think of Tom's Shoes, a company that prides itself as the "original one for one" corporation. You buy a pair for yourself, and the firm gives a pair to someone in need in another part of the world. If you have seen the emotionally moving Iranian movie *Children of Heaven* (1997), you can imagine how prized a pair of shoes can be for children in poor communities. So, a gift attached to your purchase of a pair of Tom's

Figure 6 Rina Sawayama performs live on the main stage at the Reading Festival 2023.

Photo by Simone Joyner/Getty Images

> Rina Sawayama is one of the young artists who is unafraid of using her art to tackle issues such as biphobia, racism, and consumerism. Sawayama's 2020 song 'XS' holds up a mirror to a society steeped in mindless consumption. In her own words, "'XS' is a song that mocks capitalism in a sinking world. Given that we all know global climate change is accelerating and human extinction is a very real possibility within our lifetime it seemed hilarious to me that brands were still coming out with new makeup palettes every month and public figures were doing a gigantic house tour of their gated property in Calabasas in the same week as doing a 'sad about Australian wild fires' Instagram post."[46]

Shoes makes a lot of common sense. In the context of sustainability, Starbucks does that by convincing its patrons that consumption of Starbucks coffee is like investing into "coffee ethics"—a sustainable and fair system of coffee farming.

Zizek argues that such ethical consumption can simply "prolong the disease," by effectively detracting a conscientious consumer from investigating the fundamental reasons why a large population in the world struggles to afford a pair of shoes or why growing coffee is unremunerative for coffee farmers and therefore unsustainable in the long run. The rhetoric of sustainability sucks ethically minded consumers into sustaining the status quo. The chimera of ethical consumption provides a Band-Aid as a substitute for surgery needed to address structural inequalities.

By Way of a Conclusion: Is Just Sustainability Viable?

The concept of sustained yield that German foresters had developed, and colonial forest administrators proselytized to people in other parts of the world has been applied to other resources and sectors, for example, "sustainable Moringa," "sustainable fisheries," "sustainable palm," and "sustainable tourism." A few of these initiatives have produced some social benefits and have contributed to resource conservation. However, the narratives of win-win sustainability have not helped the long-term goals of environmental stewardship. Instead, they have set us back by blunting the force of our resolve to radically reduce consumption and conserve resources. Moreover, just as the discourses of "sustainable forestry" have led to the dispossession of forest-dependent people in the Global South, initiatives in sustainable fisheries and sustainable tourism have often increased the burden on the poor.[47] In other cases, sustainability draws on the 'environmental labor' of working classes, who make do without living wages and other types of social protections.[48] In essence, win-lose processes have been sold as win-win, mainly by the winners committed to sustaining the status quo.

Despite these problems, there have been remarkable attempts to rescue sustainability from its technocratic and managerial versions.

First, environmental politics and policy scholars have proposed a classification of weak versus strong sustainability. Weak sustainability involves attempts to tinker with the status quo to pursue a technocratic balance between environment and development, which has mostly failed. Strong sustainability seeks a fundamental transformation of the social, political, and economic systems around the ideas of justice and fairness. These proposals are aspirations worth pursuing but the viability of these plans is questionable as the following reflections from another group engaged in a similar exercise show.

Environmental justice activists in the United States have long argued that sustainable development cannot be achieved without securing social and environmental justice. A group of scholar activists, including Bob Bullard, Julian Agyeman, and Vanesa Castán Broto have sought to embed sustainability within stronger emphases on social justice and precautionary principles. For them, sustainability entails "the need to ensure a better quality of life for all, now, and into the future, in a just and equitable manner, while living within the limits of supporting ecosystems."[49] They have come up with the phrase "just sustainabilities" to signify this union of environmental sustainability and social justice. Others have sought to "situate" sustainability vis-à-vis the differences of geography, race, gender, and class, among others.[50]

We recognize the value of these proposals, especially because they come from a group of scholar activists who have joined hands and stood shoulder to shoulder with racial minorities and other marginalized communities fighting for environmental justice. Yet, these scholars acknowledge that "the linkages between the ideas of sustainability and environmental justice are clearer with respect to the *problems* identified by our authors than the *solutions* currently possible within dominant social paradigm."[51] Such an acknowledgment by these authors is indicative of the central problem we have identified with the concepts of sustainability and sustainable development.

These concepts were not designed to prioritize environmental stewardship. They were invented to ensure a stable supply of natural resources for those whose business was to maintain high levels of resource extraction. This often fundamentally changed the nature of the resource; for example, old growth natural forests were reduced to monocrop plantations. Integrating social justice into sustainable development, as proponents of strong sustainability argue, while eminently desirable, seems to be a far cry in the face of the enduring attraction, power, and obsession with technical solutions that make sustainability so popular.

The claim we advance here is thus different from the problem that social justice activists often identify vis-à-vis sustainability. They argue that sustainability prioritizes concerns that are exclusively "environmental," while ignoring the concerns of equity. We argue that in the long run, sustainability and sustainable development do not even serve the goals of environmental conservation. Part of the problem relates to the hegemony of market-oriented approaches to environment and development.

Sustainability works well for those whose interests align with market-based and technology-driven proposals for environmental protection. Green consumption, responsible consumerism, or other variants under the umbrella of sustainability eventually cannot help because of their umbilical links to capitalism. Perpetual growth, rising profits, and increasing accumulation are not aberrations in contemporary capitalism that can be addressed. They are its soul, and capitalism cannot exist without these features.[52] Therefore, any form of sustainable production, consumption, and exchange will eventually either transform to enable and accelerate the accumulation of capital or will have to die. It is for this reason that we argue that decolonizing environmentalism requires that we abandon the hope placed in ideas such as sustainable development and sustainability. Instead, we should step back, train our political energies to dislodge consumerism, think deeply about degrowth, and develop new imaginations of a just and healthy planet.

In the next chapter, we shift our attention to another type of response that proponents of mainstream environmentalism have articulated. These responses address criticism that environmental policies in general, and conservation in particular, have either ignored or violated the traditional rights of Indigenous communities, and that their traditional knowledge has been devalued and marginalized. These criticisms have triggered myriad actions and reforms within global conservation programs. Yet, as we show in the next chapter, these shifts are usually limited to hyperbole and patronizing notions of "inclusion" without making fundamental changes to the status quo.

How Not to Decolonize: Instrumentalizing Indigenous Rights and Wisdom

The last few years have seen a significant upsurge in the celebration of Indigenous cultures and wisdom in the Global North. This includes valuing their knowledge systems, environmentally friendly rituals, livelihoods and lifestyles, and above all their belief in the unity of nature and society. This recognition follows a long history of colonization of Indigenous Nations, forced assimilation, violent land grabs, and genocide. In the past, Indigenous Peoples have been treated as inferior, unfit to learn from, and inconsequential in the larger scheme of environmentalism. Since the turnaround, paying homage to the wisdom of Indigenous Peoples has become a new ritual in global debates on the environment and climate. However, these ritualized homages are yet to translate into substantive engagement with Indigenous communities, their contributions to environmental stewardship, and Indigenous sovereignty. What are the drivers of these conflicting tendencies within environmental and climate circles? Why do big environmental NGOs go overboard in celebrating Indigenous cultures, only to resort to corporate greenwashing partnerships that lead to violation of Indigenous rights? Here, we distill core insights from a long history of exchanges between mainstream environmentalism and Indigenous groups to draw lessons for contemporary debates on the environmental and climate crises.

Indigenous Stewardship of Nature

Scientific studies show that Indigenous Peoples, and other rural communities throughout the Global South have nurtured the soil, landscape, and natural forests through their farming practices and other engagements with their environments. For example, archeologists have found that subsistence agriculture enriched degraded landscapes that host some of the best rainforests in the Amazon.[1] This phenomenon is popularly known as the Amazonian dark earths. A multidisciplinary group of scientists has reported a similar phenomenon in West Africa, which they call "African Dark Earths." Their research shows that "the ancient methods of adding charcoal and kitchen waste to highly weathered, nutrient poor tropical soils can transform the land into enduringly fertile, carbon-rich black soils."[2] Yet, a narrow, colonial mentality and racial prejudices have hindered the recognition of these contributions. Instead, large sections of the scientific and environmental community blame rural and Indigenous populations for environmental degradation. For example, David Attenborough's speech at the release of the influential *Dasgupta Review* in February 2021 portrayed members of local communities as short-sighted, arguing that they could not help but cut rainforest down, while "people across the world" (Read, the privileged in the Global North) valued them for their contribution to climate stability.[3]

Fortunately, strong advocacy by Indigenous rights groups and rural community organizations has brought these debates into national and global policy arenas. Various multilateral agencies, such as the World Bank and the United Nations have come up with codes of conduct, guidelines, and declarations recognizing these rights. These include the UN Declaration on the Rights of Indigenous Peoples (UNDRIP), and the UN Declaration on the Rights of Peasants and Other People Working in Rural Areas (UNDROP). These are important instruments, with potentially consequential benefits in the long run. However, it is important to recognize that these instruments are non-binding in nature. The task of enforcing their provisions falls back on national governments and international actors, who have a history of violating the rights of Indigenous and other local communities across the world.[4]

The authors of *Reserved! Indigenous Peoples facing Nature Conservation* found that even amongst countries with legal recognition of Indigenous Peoples' land rights, conflicts over forest and land rights persist.[5] Another recent study found that industrial projects threaten nearly 60 percent of Indigenous lands worldwide, with the planned expansion of renewable energy infrastructure, including solar, wind, and hydro-electric projects, threatening 42 percent of Indigenous territories.[6] These threats add to the long-standing phenomenon of appropriation of Indigenous territories to set aside protected areas that are managed as a fortress—often with the coercive force of fines, fences, and firearms.[7] A deeper understanding of the paradoxical spike in threats to Indigenous territories, despite a quarter-century-long history of the publicly stated commitment to Indigenous rights by international agencies and conservation NGOs, demands a nuanced understanding of the history and intellectual foundations of global conservation, to which we turn next.

"Ecologically Noble Indian": Colonial Legacies and Continued Contradictions

Global conservation's founding fathers portrayed Indigenous People as "primitives." Sierra Club founder John Muir described Native Americans and Black people as dirty, lazy, and uncivilized. In a collection of essays published in 1901 to promote national parks, he assured prospective tourists, "As to Indians, most of them are dead or civilized into useless innocence."[8] Similarly, racism drove advocacy by European conservationists and colonial forestry administrations who sought to include in protected areas "savages," "primitives," "Naturvölker," "hunter-gatherers," and "ecosystem peoples."[9] Tanganyika's (erstwhile Tanzania) National Park Board of Trustees wrote in 1955 that the Serengeti region was *reserved as a natural habitat both for the game and human beings in their primitive state.*"[10] Most National Parks in the United States and other parts of the world were carved out of the territories that European settlers grabbed via violence or deceit. This history is captured at length in Mark Dowie's pathbreaking global study of tens of millions "conservation refugees" who have been left homeless because their homelands were declared wildlife reserves.[11] Dispossession of Indigenous Americans continued even after the parks were established and some of the famed conservationists vouched for the value of Indigenous-American culture. Research by environmental and Indigenous-American historians shows that the white superintendents of newly established national parks sought to make these areas "safe" by removing "primitive savages" from the park boundaries.[12]

These writings constitute the tip of a proverbial iceberg of the deep history of conflicts between European conservationists and Indigenous and other people living in rural and forest areas in colonized countries. Some scholars and advocates of conservation discount these histories as a reflection of the predominant values of an era gone by. These claims are refuted by the persistence of colonial-era narratives in contemporary debates. In particular, it is instructive to see how ecologists have continued to reproduce discourses of the ecologically noble Indian, also referred in an uncharitable framing of "ecologically noble savages."

An authoritative review of *The Ecologically Noble Savage Debate*, published in the prestigious *Annual Review of Anthropology*, offers an insightful observation. The irony of this review is that the author entirely misses the point of critical scholarship on "ecological savages" or "noble savages." Instead, he takes these phrases as objective truths and subjects them to empirical scrutiny. The extent of crass empiricism underlying the review is evident in the conclusions that the author draws: "Following *a strict definition of conservation* as advocated by behavioral ecologists and conservation biologists, one can conclude that conservation by native peoples is uncommon."[13] Subjecting this deeply problematic "debate" on "ecologically noble savages" to the most reductionist and distorted forms of empiricism is a sad commentary on some sections of academia steeped in a technocratic and decontextualized understanding of environmental conservation.

At first one wonders if the author of this review was narrowly focused on technical research in ecology, perhaps ignorant of the research on the sociology and politics of stereotyping Indigenous Peoples. But the review mentions a strand of this debate that is "broader and more humanistic and political in orientation and considers the concept of ecological nobility in terms of identity, ecological knowledge, and ideology."[14] However, instead of engaging with the debate, the author criticizes these arguments as "odd additions" to the debate.[15] Yet, the author engages in a similar argument by suggesting that conservation organizations "used" Indigenous Peoples "to advance the organizations' agenda."[16] The author mentions how these organizations "paraded" Indigenous representatives at environmental conferences as authentic noble savages who knew the secrets of effective conservation. This was designed to ensure fundraising as it corresponded to preexisting values of first-world donors and their supporters.[17] Despite these critical observations, the author fails to draw implications for how ecologists may also be viewing Indigenous cultures and wisdoms instrumentally. Instead, the author selectively cites each strand of the scholarship to gravitate to a pre-determined argument to invalidate any claims regarding Indigenous stewardship of nature.

This is surprising because in many cases biologists have acknowledged diverse social constructs of biodiversity. One study found that plural understandings of the "notions of balance, food chains, and human–nature interactions ..." was "strongly related to their attitudes toward best practices in managing biodiversity."[18] A respect for the plurality of values and understandings of conservation among young conservation researchers led a group of interdisciplinary scientists to caution against promoting "a single philosophy" as a silver bullet for successful conservation.[19] However, such pleas have gone unheeded as big international environmental NGOs (BINGOs) continue to promote myths of pristine conservation that require fencing out local communities of Indigenous and other forest-dependent peoples. This authoritarian view of how to do "global conservation" has led to recurring and widespread conflicts, which undermine the lives and livelihoods of Indigenous Peoples and contribute to grave human rights violations.[20]

Well over three decades of advocacy for addressing these conflicts have yielded little gains. For example, the Coordinating Body of Indigenous Organizations of the Amazon Basin (COICA) released a statement to "the community of concerned environmentalists" in 1989 to propose an alliance "in defense of our Amazonian homeland."[21] COICA representatives noted that the conservationists had "left … the Indigenous Peoples, out of [their] vision of the Amazonian Biosphere." These and other efforts at calling attention to ongoing conflicts triggered by global conservation were well documented in a highly influential essay by anthropologist Mac Chapin. Chapin documented off-the-record deliberations at a June 2003 meeting of representatives from major foundations and charities supporting biodiversity. They had assembled in South Dakota for a meeting of the Consultative Group on Biodiversity.

The deliberations led to an influential foundation commissioning a study for analyzing the implications of the rapid growth of BINGOs that had become extremely wealthy in a short period of time. More worryingly, their approach to conservation "evoked a number of questions—and complaints—from local communities, national NGOs and human rights activists."[22] Apparently, these reports had been censored by the influential conservation leaders who sat on the board of the foundations that commissioned these studies. Chapin waited for a full year and only after the Consultative Group on

Biodiversity had convened once again in June 2004 in Minnesota, he made his analysis public. The question of conservation-induced conflicts came up again, but as one participant put it, "they went around and around and around, without resolving anything."[23]

The intransigence and self-centered approaches of conservation groups vindicated the alarm raised at the International Forum on Indigenous Mapping in Vancouver, British Columbia, in the spring of 2004. Some 200 Indigenous delegates assembled at this forum signed a declaration stating that "conservation [had] become the number one threat to indigenous territories."[24] Such multipronged and increasingly loud backlash against global conservation groups accused of numerous violations of the rights of Indigenous Peoples forced BINGOs to recognize the problem. In response, conservation groups and their global supporters commissioned a number of studies, reports, and initiatives celebrating Indigenous Peoples' role in conservation. In the following section, we offer a careful analysis of these reports, which suggests that hidden beneath the glib narratives of respecting Indigenous rights lies a strategy of instrumentalizing Indigenous culture in the service of fundamentally exclusionary models of global conservation.

BINGO! Big International NGOs and the Narrative of Indigenous "Rights"

Backlash at the beginning of the new millennium led a number of global conservation groups—including Bird Life International, Conservation International, Fauna & Flora International, the Nature Conservancy, the International Union for the Conservation of Nature (IUCN), the Wildlife Conservation Society, and the World Wide Fund for Nature (WWF)—to join hands in 2009 to form the Conservation Initiative on Human Rights (CIHR). CIHR seeks to improve the practice of conservation by promoting the integration of human rights in conservation policy and practice.[25] Some of the most prominent BINGOs also launched the paradigm of Rights-based Approach (RBA) to conservation. A report commissioned by the IUCN defines RBAs "as integrating rights norms, standards, and principles into policy, planning, implementation, and outcomes assessment to help ensure that conservation practice respects rights in all cases and supports their further realization where possible."[26] Another report equates RBAs to "conservation with justice," which "puts an emphasis on conservation but *highlights the livelihoods and rights aspects* of projects, programs, and activities."[27]

We've decided to compromise. We keep the land, the mineral rights, natural resources, fishing and timber, and in return we'll acknowledge you as the traditional owners of it.

Figure 7 Statements of intent to "recognize and respect" the rights of Indigenous Peoples are commonplace, yet the assault on Indigenous territories, resources, and culture continues unabated. As Indigenous leaders and scholars have argued, decolonization is often reduced to rhetoric without investing in restoring the material and political conditions necessary for Indigenous sovereignty.

Cartoon by Malcolm McGookin/Cartoonstock UK

These initiatives, reports, conference panels, and press conferences have led to constant reiteration of Indigenous rights over natural resources, a strategy that seems to be extremely popular among both advocates of Indigenous rights and BINGOs. Yet little seems to have changed, as the violation of the rights of Indigenous People continues, documented recently by a group of scholar-activists led by UN Special Rapporteur Victoria Tauli-Corpuz.[28] As discussed in the previous chapter, Credible evidence of human rights violations from over a dozen conservation projects prompted the German government agencies and the US Fish and Wildlife Department to stop funding some of the most prominent BINGOs. It is evident that there is a fundamental disconnect between the popular narratives of respect for Indigenous rights and the reality of mainstream environmentalism, even today. We argue that this disconnect has escaped the attention of all but a few critical analysts. To reveal these gaps, it is useful to probe deeper into the pro-Indigenous narrative before dwelling on the historical roots of this narrative.

Consider the article *Indigenous people and nature: a tradition of conservation* published under the Ecosystems and Biodiversity section on the webpage of UN Environment:

> In the culture of the Maori people of New Zealand, humans are deeply connected with nature; the two are equal and interdependent, even kin … The Maoris' intimate relationship with their lands and the natural world is shared by many other indigenous peoples around the world and highlights why these often marginalized groups are gaining recognition as vital stewards of our environment and its fast-depleting resources.[29]

After a quick reference to the Māori People, the article shifts to a broad generalization of Indigenous People the world over. They are represented as "stout opponents of development imposed from beyond their communities," who "defend their lands against illegal encroachments and destructive exploitation." Overall, the article presents and reinforces the binaries of environment and development—"good environment" pitted against "bad development." The narrative of good environment is paused momentarily to discuss how "the United States" famed national parks' have "excluded" Indigenous peoples "from ancestral lands across the planet in the name of protecting nature." And that "conservation groups who backed this approach *stand accused* of creating millions of conservation refugees."[30]

All of this sugarcoats the reality that even in the twentieth and twenty-first centuries, global conservation advocacy has created new enclosures dispossessing millions of members of Indigenous and other rural communities, who have been robbed of their land, resources, and cultures. Yet the UNEP report does not use this discussion to scrutinize dominant models of conservation, pivoting instead to the assertion that "conservationists have come to understand that the landscapes they considered 'wilderness' have been influenced and protected by local and indigenous communities, and that these groups have useful knowledge on how to manage them." There is little scrutiny of the dominant model of conservation. These rhetorical strategies and narrative styles are repeated in nearly all of the major reports on the discussion of Indigenous Peoples within the context of global conservation. Consider another example from WWF, celebrating the International Day of the World Indigenous Peoples on August 9th:

> Over the decades, conservation by governments or conservation organizations has been regarded as the only legitimate form of conservation. *In some cases, conservation of protected areas equaled exclusion of people* and empty nature, a view of conservation devoid of human components.[31]

WWF uses the vocabulary of incidental and exceptional exclusion of people to obfuscate ongoing dispossessions. The article later describes that "inclusive conservation initiatives depend on the strength of the communities themselves ('how strong and committed we are')." The article concludes by spelling out WWF's intention to support "indigenous conservation" by way of "recognition, information, and capacity building to enable Indigenous and local communities to be *responsible participants* and champions of inclusive conservation in Indonesia and the world."[32] Instead of scrutinizing the actions and strategies of powerful conservation actors, WWF shifts the onus of inclusive conservation on local communities. Yet, WWF is not alone in this practice.

Instead of seeking or building on already existing independent research, each of the BINGOs commissioned reports to valorize Indigenous People's contribution to nature conservation and outlined lofty visions of protecting Indigenous rights. An extensive independent review of all major reports and statements of solidarity with Indigenous People issued by conservation organizations revealed a curious contradiction within these declarations of "rights-based approaches to conservation."[33] These documents list an expansive set of rights, for example, "rights of territorial sovereignty," only to reduce these rights to an instrument for serving the goals of nature conservation set unilaterally by global conservation groups. None of these reports list any meaningful criteria by which the actions of conservation actors could be scrutinized for their effect on Indigenous rights. No criteria or conditions are outlined when conservation projects must be stopped to protect community rights. When conservation programs run into conflicts with Indigenous rights, instead of entering into deliberations with Indigenous Peoples' organizations, the resolution of potential conflicts is left to the discretion of local employees of global conservation NGOs.[34]

In a nutshell, despite the rhetoric of rights-based approaches, conservation actors have made no efforts to institutionalize accountability for their actions. However, superficial celebrations of Indigenous sovereignty by conservation NGOs are deployed as a virtue-signaling tactic, while masking the systemic and structural imbalances of power between local communities and global conservation NGOs, which has led to recurring violations of human rights.

In 2016 Survival International, an international Indigenous advocacy group, filed a 228-page formal complaint to the Organization for Economic Co-operation and Development (OECD), alleging that "anti-poaching eco-guards who were part-funded and logistically helped by WWF, victimized the hunter-gatherer Baka people, razed to the ground their camps, destroyed or confiscated their property, forced them to relocate and have regularly used physical force and threats of violence against them."[35] The year after, an investigative report by BBC revealed that wildlife rangers in India's Kaziranga National Park renowned for its endemic and endangered population of one-horned rhinos had killed more than fifty people, most of them poor Adivasis—India's Indigenous People—over a three-year period on suspicion of being poachers. These rangers had shoot-to-kill orders from officers in government forestry agencies which were funded by the WWF. The WWF also provides specialist equipment including night vision goggles used in the park's anti-poaching efforts. Instead of refuting these charges, a WWF official defended these actions: "Nobody is comfortable with killing people … What is needed is on the ground protection. The poaching has to stop."[36] This statement came from Dr. Dipankar Ghose, who is protected not only by his employment by WWF, but also by the social privileges he enjoys as an upper caste male in India. These privileges afford him the audacity to make these bold statements without the fear of any repercussions for what Survival International refers to as "extra-judicial killings."

Despite high-profile investigative reportage by the BBC, the WWF or the forestry agencies hardly faced any scrutiny in India. The country's federal environmental ministry, which has long been involved in similar violations of *Adivasi* (Indigenous) lives and livelihoods, defended its state agencies and the WWF. A similar investigation by Buzzfeed in 2019 exposed shocking instances of violent abuse by Ecoguards and rangers inside Nepal's renowned Chitwan National Park. The park warden was charged with "torturing (an apparently innocent) man to death," which prompted WWF's Nepal staff to lobby for the charges to disappear. After the Nepalese government dropped the case a few months later, WWF declared it as an indication of "a victory in the fight against poaching."[37] This was not surprising given that Buzzfeed reported that WWF, "funds, equips, and works directly with [government] forces that have tortured, raped and killed people." This prompted the German government to freeze its funding of the WWF project in July 2019.[38] Subsequently, in October 2020, the US government's Fish and Wildlife Department also stopped over $12 million of funding to WWF, the Wildlife Conservation Society (WCS) and other conservation NGOs, following a bipartisan investigation into whether conservation funds meant for anti-poaching activities were tied to human rights abuses in African nations.[39]

To be clear, violations of human rights in conservation projects are not a case of isolated failures. The twenty-first-century global conservation is significantly more militarized as compared to the nineteenth-century colonial conservation. Elizabeth Lunstrum coined the concept of "green militarization," for the "use of military and paramilitary personnel, training, technologies, and partnerships in the pursuit of conservation efforts."[40] Rosaleen Duffy and colleagues show that militarization of conservation is especially rampant in Africa.[41] This involves foreign ex-military personnel, private contractors, serving soldiers, and local army veterans working across Africa as various kinds of "conservation armies."[42] Militarization of conservation is institutionalized in the form of 2014 London Declaration on the Illegal Wildlife Trade, which seeks to strengthen law enforcement to curb poaching. Philanthropic foundations and government agencies often advocate for the allocation of resources to wildlife enforcement as the income from wildlife poaching could be used to fund violent militias and Islamist terrorism in parts of the African continent.[43]

Conservation social scientists scrutinize how international and national agencies define poachers and the extent to which militarized approaches indicate conservationists' willingness to engage in "coercive, repressive policies that are ultimately counterproductive."[44] Researchers have also questioned the validity of the narrowly conceptualized "poacher-as-terrorist" master-narrative, which obscures the many complex reasons for regional insecurity and losses of biodiversity. They argue that these narratives distract from the local victims of terrorist violence, for example, mobile pastoralists, while contributing to further environmental degradation.[45] Commentators who recognize the potential links between poaching and terrorism also show that the terrorism–poaching nexus is frequently exaggerated by national security agencies and other powerful actors, who benefit from illegal trafficking of wildlife.[46] The poaching–terrorism links are part of a broader phenomenon in which powerful actors exploit the narratives for vested interests while deflecting attention away from the violent implications of the militarization of conservation.

Recent research suggests that the intensification of "militarized conservation" is being sold to individual supporters, who seem to directly fund specific spectacularized militarized interventions, a phenomenon that scholars describe as "militarization by consumption."[47] Consumption of wildlife products for their supposed aphrodisiac properties in parts of East Asia is often blamed for poaching, yet research shows that this explanation may be rooted in colonial stereotypes about horny Asian men.[48] Large-scale trophy hunting by European colonizers, which continues to be promoted in the name of supporting conservation, and large markets for wildlife products in Western societies are much bigger triggers for wildlife poaching.[49] Capitalism has become a major force in commercializing wildlife, including through the phenomenon of trophy hunting.[50] However, popular media and wildlife conservation groups often ignore these root causes, which hides the role that affluence and luxury consumption play in wildlife poaching.[51]

More broadly, conservation NGOs have become an important focus of corporate social responsibility interventions. Conservation NGOs argue that these partnerships help mitigate the negative environmental effects of corporate activities while supporting conservation projects. Yet, most such partnerships had "limited positive effect on biodiversity conservation."[52] There is increasing evidence to suggest that many, if not most, of these conservation–corporate partnerships end up in some form of greenwashing.[53] Such conflict of interest on the part of conservation NGOs cast conservation-related human rights violations in an even murkier light. Having engaged with this issue for nearly two decades, we believe that global conservation will not reform until it is heavily regulated by an international mechanism that takes the rights of Indigenous Peoples and other rural communities seriously. These regulations however must be preceded by purging global conservation of its neocolonial and racist underpinnings. A careful analysis of the multifaceted nature of Indigenous Peoples' engagement with nature is crucial to counter the myriad forms of simplified abstractions that BINGOs craft about Indigenous contributions to conservations.

Demystifying Indigenous Engagements with the Environment

The essentialization and instrumentalization of Indigenous knowledge in the service of global conservation are rooted in colonial views about Indigenous Peoples. Such a caricatured view of Indigenous wisdom fails to see Indigenous lifestyles as part of a broader sociocultural and economic system. As anthropologist Paul Nadasdy argues, while participants in the debate on ecologically noble Indian have scrutinized cultural assumptions underlying Euro-American notions of indigenousness, they are yet to scrutinize "the equally problematic concepts of environmentalism and conservation," steeped in Euro–American culture.[54] Nadasdy argues that ecologists and other actors, with apparently good intentions, have sought to fit Indigenous culture and lifestyle on a spectrum of environmentalism that ranges from non-environmentalists on the one end to radical environmentalists on the other end, with "reform environmentalists" located in the middle. This spectrum of environmentalism, detached from the lived experiences of human communities, is a specific "cultural construction," rooted deeply in "Euro-American assumptions about the range of possible relationships between humans and the environment."[55]

In many cases, Indigenous groups and movements may articulate their concerns in the vocabulary that resonates with influential actors. Yet, that should not be taken to mean that Indigenous Peoples and their engagement with nature are restricted to cultural and spiritual realms alone. Nature is intertwined with all spheres of Indigenous People's lives—they hunt, farm, and engage in controlled burning of fields, which is part of an agroecological approach to farming. The use of fire is not just a ritual, which is why it is a bit limiting to showcase the Indigenous use of fire only as "cultural burning."[56] Accordingly, the first important step for environmentalists interested in engaging with Indigenous wisdom on environmentalism is to recognize that for Indigenous Peoples, nature or the environment is not just an object of aesthetic or spiritual interest, but a material reality integral to their lives and lifeworlds.

The lives and livelihoods of Indigenous Peoples have evolved over generations as a result of conscious efforts to thrive in an environment rich in natural resources. However, the dispossession of Indigenous

Peoples through colonialism, imperialism, and extractive capitalism has been so severe that it has often ruptured their relationships with their environments. Leaders of the Yurok tribe in northern California wrote in their 1993 constitution, "Our social and ecological balance, thousands and thousands of years old, was shattered by the invasion of the non-Indians."[57] Under these changed circumstances, many Indigenous Peoples have taken on economic activities that may not necessarily produce environmentally favorable outcomes. In that sense, in addition to addressing the effects of settler colonialism, these Indigenous communities must also deal with the challenges that everyone else in the world confronts today. Those challenges and the need for supporting them through reparations are minimized when Indigenous Peoples are painted in a simplistic and essentialized way as people who live in an essential and static harmony with nature.

Tribal sovereignty within the constitutional framework of the United States means that for many Indigenous Nations, the main issue is regaining control over their territories and an ability to exercise sovereignty in managing their territory and resources. As Perry H. Charley of the Navajo Nation, who is the director and senior scientist at Diné College's Environmental Outreach and Research Institute, says, "We are a nation within a nation ... We have our own laws, and it is up to us to be vigilant in those."[58] Indeed, several Indigenous Nations within the United States and Canada have decided against some extractive projects, while signing on to others. Such conundrums are clearly illustrated in the case of the Missouri River Resources (MRR), a tribal-owned oil company with the motto "Sovereignty by the Barrel." The motto refers to a change in status from when the tribe had leased the majority of tribal lands to private companies, who drilled for oil and paid the tribe 18 percent royalties, which has increased to 26 percent since MRR started drilling on its own.[59] The increased income in the hands of tribal government can help strengthen infrastructure, improved human development indicators, and safety cushions for absorbing negative consequences of resource exploitation. At the same time, local community groups, such as Fort Berthold POWER (Protectors of Water and Earth Rights), are striving to hold MMR to regulatory standards and are calling for health and environmental impact studies just like they did while holding Big Oil accountable.[60]

Another insightful case is the Yurok tribe's sale of hundred-year contracts for forest carbon offsets under California's cap-and-trade program. This additional income has enabled them to buy back nearly 80,000 acres of their traditional territory.[61] It is difficult to argue against the tribe's engagement with a neoliberal carbon offset program when it has directly helped them restore their traditional territories, perhaps the most powerful decolonizing measure one can think of. These cases show that opposition to extractive or neoliberal development and climate projects is not a necessary feature of all Indigenous communities. In some cases, Indigenous Peoples and their elected representative may also choose to embrace settler colonial institutions and solutions. The constitutional framework that recognizes territorial sovereignty of Indigenous Nations and the fundamental integrity of the rule of law framework in northern America affords Indigenous Peoples in the United States and Canada some level of autonomy in decision-making. In other parts of the world, Indigenous rights are barely recognized and are violated with impunity.[62]

A carbon offset program like the one the Yurok tribe used to buy back their historical territory could also be designed in India or other countries. Government agencies in India claim to have put in place the policy framework needed for capitalizing such global carbon offset programs to aid local development and contribute to the goals of addressing the climate crisis. However, studies show that Indian government agencies have exploited these programs to capture resources for the bureaucracy in government forestry agencies.[63] Under the specific institutional context in India, the missing mechanisms of public accountability, and a failure of the rule of law, government agencies are reasserting control over Indigenous lands leading to a new wave of dispossessions. As a result, while the same neoliberal carbon offset programs can be implemented in some parts of the world to the benefit of Indigenous Peoples and other marginalized groups, historically entrenched inequalities mean that these programs can be exploited more blatantly by political and economic elites in other contexts.[64]

The comparative differences in vulnerability of Indigenous Peoples and rural communities across the world are a reminder that the disadvantages experienced by marginalized groups cannot be addressed just by recognizing and respecting their knowledge and wisdom. Addressing these historically accumulated and deeply entrenched injustices requires significant structural reforms at international, national, and subnational levels. The United Nations Declaration on the Rights of Indigenous Peoples (UNDRIP) adopted in 2007, and the United Nations Declaration on the Rights of Peasants and Other People Working in Rural Areas (UNDROP), adopted in 2018, both seek to rectify historical injustices. These are important beginnings, but insufficient for redressing widespread injustices.[65] Bringing about transformative change in the status quo requires attention to both the underlying intellectual foundations and the structural manifestations of mainstream environmentalism.

Conclusion: Toward Anti-Racist Models of Living with Nature

The plethora of ongoing attempts to essentialize Indigenous Peoples "environmentalism is borne out of neither a sociological understanding of their life worlds nor from the intent to empower them. Instead, rhetorical campaigns celebrating Indigenous Peoples" rights are designed for coopting the narratives of Indigenous rights to serve a specific type of environmental imaginary rooted in settler colonial conservation. National Parks and Wildlife Reserves—sanitized enclosures—are meant for dazzling well-paying tourists while offering tokenistic respect for nature. These enclosures, coupled with monocultures of industrial forestry, have greatly exacerbated the risks of large-scale pest attacks and catastrophic forest fires. In contrast, productive uses of landscapes for subsistence farming, small-scale animal husbandry, fishing, and subsistence hunting foster deeper engagement.

Indigenous and many rural cultures around the world demonstrate the viability of a connected human-natural world, which is the opposite of the fortress conservation models promoted by BINGOs and adopted by governments the world over. An anti-racist model of conservation should be aimed at dismantling the monopoly of BINGOs on global conservation. This would require redirecting resources away from the wealthiest and biggest conservation NGOs— some of which raise close to a billion dollars a year and employ thousands of workers. The conservation industry, as it is referred to by many in the field, organizes "the Business of Conservation" conferences with hefty registration fees and corporate-style galas.[66] Conservation funds should be redirected to grassroots groups doing the hard job of aiding local conservation efforts.[67] One such example is Tanzania's Land Conservancies, which steward wildlife on land that is collectively owned and managed by local communities. Some of these conservancies are led by women leaders.[68]

The most precious insight from Indigenous cultures is to show that an entire lifeworld can be built around meaningful engagements with nature. Such a vision goes beyond the settler colonial vocabulary of sustainable materialism, which is presented as an empty abstraction that seeks to mimic "the material practices of environmental activism," without being grounded in "the actual embodied, interactive, emplaced, and networked practices at stake ..."[69] An anti-racist environmentalism should be based on specific, place-based, emancipatory, and regenerative practices that help build and strengthen nature-society bonds.[70] However, as scholars of global conservation have argued, our imagination of anti-racist and regenerative environmentalism must go beyond celebrating local environmentalism. As Aby Sène argues, upholding the rights to self-determination of Black and Indigenous Peoples' demands that global conservation unshackles itself from capitalism and the racial order that sustains it.[71] While these demands are often recognized, they are often appropriated to promote progressive blueprints that are rooted in the specificities of Western capitalism. This leads to the erasure of the agency of BIPOC communities and scholars, whose voices and insights are diminished and instrumentalized to propagate the dominant modes of thinking and acting.[72] At the same time, many scholars and writers seek to amplify BIPOC voices and insights without falling into the trap of appropriation. Liz Carlisle chronicles "the stories of Black, Latinx, and Asian American farmers who are ... restoring native prairies, nurturing beneficial fungi, and enriching soil health."[73] These stories enliven the possibilities of "stitching ecosystems back together," while nurturing family histories and community.

The second important element of an anti-racist conservation is its collective dimension, grounded in the sovereignty of a people to control their destiny and practice homegrown ethos. This means conceptualizing the protection of nature as "a political battle" grounded in Black political ecology and African-centered political ecology.[74] A failure to recognize alternative epistemologies has led to a depoliticized view of co-production and participatory research, which focuses on narrowly defined methodological questions.[75] Three, none of these transformative changes can be ushered in through some sort of programmatic agenda. As we discuss in Chapter 7, these battles must be led by emancipatory environmental and social movements, and this battle must engage global youth movements. The next chapter discusses two such prominent movements that are potential allies on the path to decolonizing environmentalism.

Youth Climate Movements: Accomplishments, Challenges, and Transformations

On August 20, 2018, an unknown teenager decided to skip school and sit-in at the gates of the Swedish parliament. Her hand-made placard read "ScholStrejk for Klimatet." Not many in that bustling part of Stockholm paid attention. Six days later, her parents, a few teachers, and some friends from her school joined in at the next sit-in. The motley group got some media attention. By the next month, Greta Thunberg, as the world would soon know her, had begun a youth movement that spread like wildfire across the globe. Greta began a weekly strike for climate, inviting other students to join the "Fridays for Future" (FFF) campaign by walking out from classrooms every Friday.[1] By December, more than 20,000 school children from across European cities had participated in school strikes, and dozens of local chapters had started. The campaign's tech savvy supporters used social media extensively, Greta soon became a global celebrity, and the FFF went viral.[2] Over the next three months 1.6 million people from 1,700 cities across 120 countries took part in the strikes, and Greta was nominated for the Nobel Peace prize. In May 2019, Greta was featured on *Time* magazine's cover as one of the most influential persons in the world. FFF's success resulted in the first United Nations Youth Climate Summit in September 2019.[3]

Around the same time, another powerful climate movement took shape in the UK. Extinction Rebellion (XR) staged its first civil disobedience protest in London in November 2018. XR members blocked five bridges on the Thames River, disrupting rush hour traffic. That following April, XR began a mega protest across London with several thousand people occupying various parts of the city for a fortnight. These unprecedented actions brought many parts of London to a standstill. More than a thousand Londoners courted arrest, making this climate action rebellion an eye opener for spectators. Although XR was founded by veteran activists, it attracted a massive following among the youth, who were attracted to XR's demands and their style of disrupting business as usual. The youth members of XR led the London roadblocks. The youthful energy of these street protests, and coverage in conventional media and social media helped sprout innumerable XR chapters across the globe. There are now more than 1,000 chapters and 160,000 member activists across eighty-six countries.[4] The movement has also branched out into new organizations such as XR Youth and XR Global.

Both FFF and XR have rapidly become popular among youth in several parts of the world. These climate campaigns seem to have rejuvenated interest in environmental movements that have been struggling to recruit new members, especially youth. While scholars have long bemoaned the political apathy of Generation Z seemingly occupied with Instagram, Snapchat, and TikTok, FFF, and XR have leveraged the same social media to broadcast messages, recruit participants, and execute spectacular protests. Their popularity comes from the persuasive stories that they tell. For example, FFF emphasizes the ethical dilemma of young students having to sacrifice their education to confront political and corporate leaders to act on the climate crisis. They criticize political leaders for their failure to tackle the climate crisis. At the receiving end of FFF narratives are adults, especially the rich and powerful who either profit from corporate operations or run national governments, non-profits, and multilateral organizations such as the UN. Planet Earth and future generations are the victims, while the role of protagonists is thrust upon young activists.[5] This narrative has drawn support not only from the young, but also from parents, teachers, architects, designers, and adults from nearly every sphere of society.

Similarly, disappointment and anger with the business-as-usual approach of governments, corporations, and ordinary people in general are at the heart of XR's narrative and its success at recruiting members. By choosing to disrupt something as mundane as the daily commute or shopping trips, XR seeks to remind everyone of the impending doom and jolt people's consciousness. XR draws inspiration from Gandhian models of civil disobedience, mass arrests courted by India's freedom fighters, and the shaming tactics adopted by the participants in the US Civil Rights Movement. XR uses these tactics to mobilize activists to court arrests, with the intention of packing prisons, melting the hearts of magistrates, winning over the people, and forcing governments to bring about change. Their strategy relies on evoking the charismatic character of the rebel hero, who sacrifices one's freedom for a noble collective cause.

Both these movements have attracted significant media attention, have created awareness, and spawned affiliate groups across the world. Their protests have captivated the public, and revived memories of past movements such as the anti-Jim Crow sit-ins across the American South; the student movement for free speech in France; and Feminist and Queer mobilizations across the globe. Today's youth climate movements present a cause for optimism, especially in light of the repeated and nearly universal failure of political leaders in Europe, North America, and other parts of the world to act on the climate crisis. The success of youth climate movements in drawing public attention to climate change demands a deeper engagement with their founding philosophy, their vision of the environment, and the theories of change they rely on.

In the following two sections, we survey the vision, self-image, and goals of FFF and XR, the most influential among contemporary climate movements. We do this by drawing on writings and outreach materials from the movements, as well as through commentaries from participants, allies, and observers. We also briefly engage with issues of organizational structure, representation, and strategy within these movements as far as they help understand the movements' stated visions, goals, and their limitations.

Fridays for Future (FFF)

FFF's core message—that we are ignoring science and failing to decisively respond to climate change—reflects two beliefs that seem central to the movement. The first is that "listening to and following the best available science should be at the heart of our government's policies and actions."[6] The second belief is in the efficacy of targets established in the Paris Agreement. Let us reflect on both. In a 2019 congressional hearing in Washington, DC, Greta Thunberg went on to say, "I don't want you to listen to me. I want you to listen to the scientists."[7] However, the dominance of science in FFF demands has attracted criticism. Wretched of the Earth, an alliance of BIPOC organizations from the Global South, problematizes the centering of science in a movement that should have centered victims of climate change, "you may not realize that when you focus on the science you often look past ... our histories of struggle, dignity, victory, and resilience. And you look past the vast intergenerational knowledge of unity with nature that our peoples have ..."[8]

FFF's core emphasis on the science of climate change may also be unproductive for two other reasons. The first is that scientists are just one group of people who contribute to the formation of public opinion on climate change, or any matter. In many societies, especially the United States, many ignore what science says about climate change and are instead swayed by political, commercial, or religious logics.[9] The second problem, as social psychologist Darrick Evensen points out, is that while science is good at helping understand problems and define technical solutions, it is inadequate for solving ethical problems. Science, in fact, has no ethical basis of its own to address complex issues of inequality, discrimination, or exploitation. Therefore, treating science as the gold standard for dealing with such ethical problems can only produce narrow and misplaced visions of progress and transformation.[10] Environmental philosopher Stephen Gardiner argues that the real challenge in climate change is ethical, and the "considerations of justice, rights, welfare, virtue, political legitimacy, community, and humanity's relationship to nature are at the heart of policy decisions …"[11] While it is tempting to believe that science is neutral, and scientists operate in a political or moral vacuum, a society's values "shape science at nearly every stage."[12] Historians of science argue that science has always been political, with powerful social groups and institutions deciding upon what is worth studying, how much resources should be allocated for studying legitimate problems, and how knowledge produced by scientists is used.[13]

FFF's bet on science as the panacea for climate action neglects that climate change and environmental crises, broadly speaking, are rooted in historical, political, and economic processes as well as changing relationships among nature, humans, and nonhuman species.[14] Thankfully, the increasing diversity of climate movements has brought in youth activists, whose lived experiences speak to these complexities. Vanessa Nakate, Ugandan founder of the "Rise Up" youth movement in Africa and a FFF leader, sees unfairness as the defining characteristic of the climate crisis as well as climate mitigation, "those who didn't cause the climate crisis, those who aren't responsible for the rising global emissions—they're the ones on the frontlines. They're the ones whose voices are not being listened to. And they're the ones who don't get climate finance for mitigation, or adaptation, or finance for loss and damage."[15] Mitzi Jonelle Tan, an FFF youth leader from the Philippines, has experienced first-hand how worsening typhoons in her country impact the poor with much more severity than it does privileged individuals like herself. She argues, "This isn't just about the weather and the environment. It's about justice."[16] A majority of college students in America also see climate change as an ethical issue, with only about a quarter disagreeing.[17] Young people in general and youth climate activists across the globe see justice and ethics as central to the climate change debate. The second belief central to the FFF is the efficacy of the Paris Agreement. Over the years, FFF's first demand has remained very focused on this target set in 2015—"Keep the global temperature rise below 1.5°C compared to pre-industrial levels."[18] This signals FFF's conviction that if governments and corporations abide by the Paris Agreement, the current crisis can be addressed. To help signpost progress FFF, in Germany for example, has been pressuring the government for "doable" actions such as shutting down some coal plants each year.[19] While the Paris Agreement has been rightly hailed as a symbol of global cooperation for a collective goal, it aims "to hold global temperature increase to well below 2°C above pre-industrial levels and pursue efforts to limit it to 1.5°C."[20] The 1.5°C is more of an aspiration and less of a legally binding requirement per the Paris Agreement.

As this book goes into the press, Berkley Earth, a US-based independent research group, has reported that 2023 saw average temperatures rising above 1.5°C.[21] Scientists from the European Union's Copernicus Climate Change Service reported that the past twelve months clocked in at 1.52°C (2.74°F) higher on average compared with the years between 1850 and 1900.[22] This does not mean that the Paris Agreement aspiration of 1.5°C is out of reach. However, some are calling for a rethink of priorities on global climate action. Business press quotes business leaders with energy interests, including Bill Gates, but also some climate scientists, who think that "1.5C is no longer feasible."[23] This is disheartening, given that even with the average global warming of 1.5°C, some landlocked regions of the world could warm up to 3°C.

Bolivian activist Pablo Solon worries that the Paris goal will be a death sentence for many in the Global South where regional temperatures may rise much beyond 1.5°C: "We will have to choose which children are going to live. And, of course, the children of developing countries, of the poor, are going to be the ones that will not be able to survive."[24] Similarly, while the preamble to the Paris Agreement notes the importance of "climate justice," climate activist Leon Dulce points out that it does not acknowledge issues critical for climate-vulnerable nations such as agricultural decline, natural disasters, and human rights violations.[25] Dallas Goldtooth, of the Indigenous Environmental Network, sees the Paris goals to be promising, but the mechanisms to realize them as ineffective.[26] Some climate experts echo this and argue that the Paris goals are disjointed from the actual mechanisms for containing the temperature rise to 1.5°C. The system of incentives and penalties built into the Paris Agreement are too weak to ensure adherence.[27] Some forecasts suggest that the end of the century could witness average global temperature rise by up to 3°C even if all countries honor their Paris commitments.[28]

Another set of climate activists have been arguing that a narrow focus on the 1.5°C goal has been instrumental in centering market-based climate policies and programs as the dominant mitigation strategy. Indigenous American and Canadian EJ activists argue that industries and governments, working hand in hand with financial institutions, use carbon taxes and carbon pricing "to shift costs, under-report pollution, and gain profits while legitimizing business as usual." This became evident from the United Nations climate negotiations in Glasgow (COP26), Sharm el-Sheikh (COP27), and Dubai (COP28). COP26 saw 503 fossil fuel lobbyists in attendance, and COP27 had 637 hobnobbing with decision-makers.[29] The COP28 meeting in Dubai shattered all previous records. Analysis by the Kick Big Polluters Out (KBPO), widely reported in the international press, showed that at least 2,456 fossil fuel lobbyists were granted access to the COP28 climate negotiations.[30]

Long-time environmental activists Patrick Bond and Desmond D'Sa referred to the Glasgow meeting as the "Conference of the Polluters."[31] Ozawa Bineshi Albert, from the Indigenous Climate Justice Network, sees carbon trading clauses in the COP26 declaration as deeply problematic, "corporations will be allowed to continue polluting and it's a fairy tale to think that the trade in carbon gets us out of this crisis."[32] Recent events have validated these criticisms. Shell joined a growing list of corporations including Nestle, and Gucci in distancing itself from offsets because of their failures to address climate change.[33] Reports published in the Guardian and researchers from the think tank Corporate Accountability and UC Berkley have found that the vast majority of carbon offset programs are bogus and ineffective at climate change mitigation.[34] FFF's fixation with the 1.5°C goal and science may limit the space for deep engagement with ethical and political issues at the center of the climate crisis. This has important implications for how FFF engages with climate justice movements that predate it.

Beyond these goals, FFF has also been criticized for a lack of diversity in its leadership. Former and current members have raised red flags on monopolization of leadership by Euro-American members, claiming that the movement routinely tokenized its BIPOC participants. The movement initially remained indifferent to anti-racist protests triggered by George Floyd's murder despite support for it among its members. An FFF chapter in New Zealand disbanded after it failed to respond to complaints of internal racism and a toxic atmosphere. Some leaders of the chapter expressed disappointment about it being a "racist, white-dominated space," and directed supporters to connect instead with Pacifica and Maori Indigenous environmental groups in New Zealand to continue their activism.[35]

The evolution in FFF's strategies has also faced severe criticism. While the initial school strikes began and spread informally like typical grassroots campaigns, they have increasingly become highly centralized with the growth of FFF. Anonymous participants have criticized it for leaving behind its horizontal form, and for becoming less democratic in decision-making.[36] Some observers found it to be adopting a corporate style of functioning, issuing a set of carefully crafted demands, coming up with hyper-standardized training manuals, and bureaucratized procedures for starting new chapters.[37] For example, the German chapter of the movement created a central website, a spokes-council, and standardized messages.[38] The German chapter of FFF also distanced itself from Greta Thunberg's stance to "Stand with Gaza."[39] These tensions reflect a deeper struggle within FFF, as indicated by two studies on FFF activism in Germany. One study shows that FFF has motivated a large number of youths to step into the role of "active citizens" to demand political action on climate change, which is a significant change from young people seen mainly in their role as consumers.[40] Another study concluded that "the [FFF] protestors' strong focus on science-driven politics risks to overshadow these broader societal debates, potentially stabilizing the techno-centric, apolitical, and market-driven rationale behind climate action."[41]

XR: Rebellion of the Privileged

Like FFF, XR is also a young movement that took off in 2018. Since its beginning, its campaign has centered on three main demands: governments must tell the truth about the scale of the climate and ecological crises; governments must immediately act to stop biodiversity loss and reduce emissions; and governments must leave politics behind and be led by citizen assemblies.[42] Their website explains the core philosophy in the following words: "We promote civil disobedience and rebellion because we think it is necessary- we are asking people to find their courage and to collectively do what is necessary to bring about change."[43] Roger Hallam, among XR co-founders, presents rebellion as the only way out, "whether or not this leads to the extinction of the human species largely depends upon whether revolutionary changes happen within our societies in the next decade. This is not a matter of ideology, but of simple math and physics."[44] He argued in a 2019 tweet, "*There is only one way* that leads to true self-respect and that is rebellion. Let's get to it."[45]

XR organizers, participants, and allies insist on heroic rebellion as the essence of the movement's consciousness and their main modus operandi.[46] The Birmingham chapter of XR-UK explains in a Facebook post: "A hero is an ordinary individual who finds the strength to persevere and endure in spite of overwhelming obstacles."[47] A post-protest celebration on social media declared, "HEROES!!! I am so proud of our 'Tell the Truth' Tube action today and yesterday."[48] Allies of the movement, such as British labor leader and anti-apartheid activist Peter Hain, also believe that society will eventually think about XR as heroes, "who acted to save us all at the tipping point of the climate crisis."[49] An important tactic which XR adopts is to have participants readily court mass arrests during protests. This is driven by their conviction toward the so-called 3.5 percent rule: "No regime in the 20th century managed to stand against an uprising which had the active participation of up to 3.5% of the population. In the UK, this would mean mobilizing around 2 million people."[50]

Harvard University political scientist Erica Chenoweth, who coined the 3.5 percent rule, argued against its simplistic application, cautioning that several other factors, such as "momentum, organization, strategic leadership, and sustainability—are likely as important as large-scale participation in achieving movement success," and that "most mass nonviolent movements that have succeeded have done so even without achieving 3.5% popular participation."[51]

Peace activists have also expressed concerns about the XR strategies. Tim De Christopher, long-time practitioner of civil disobedience in the United States, worries about XR's oversimplification of the problem and the solution it offers: "The reality of climate change is that it's an unthinkably complex, constantly evolving, wicked problem. To present a complex problem as simple and assert that we know what will revolutionize society undermines XR's first demand: to tell the truth about the crisis."[52] Speaking from his experience of environmental activism, De Christopher suggests that sustained movements need grounded participants who can endure "the hard slog through endless struggles, surprises, and opportunities."[53] Instead, XR insists on staging spectacular protests, glorifying the arrests and the experience of being incarcerated.

A social media post from 2018 advertised their training as an opportunity to "learn confident non-violent approaches to direct action, including non-violent communication, de-escalation techniques, and *how much fun it can be being locked up*."[54] In the initial years, XR actively helped police officers in making large number of arrests to turn their events into a success, and XR leaders would often thank the police for their role as protectors during and after protests.[55]

Figure 8 Police officers arrest an apparently gleeful Extinction Rebellion activist outside the gates of Downing Street on October 8, 2019 in London, England.

Photo by Alberto Pezzali/NurPhoto/Getty Images

These descriptions of the police and celebration of incarceration reveal the privileged status of movement leaders. While there is merit in XR's argument that protestors should think of the police as only "antagonistic facilitators" who must be subverted but not denigrated, many BIPOC participants, allies, and activists find XR's casual attitude toward courting arrests deeply problematic.[56]

Susuana Amoah, a Black British activist, finds white protestors having "so much faith in the system to be on their side and not send them to prison, or not send them to prison for long." She further reflects on underlying privileges, "And the bravery around that. People of color can't do that. It won't happen for us."[57] Wretched of the Earth, the Global South grassroots BIPOC coalition we mentioned previously wrote an open letter to XR after the 2018 protests. They problematize the strategy of arrests from the perspective of minorities, "many of us live with the risk of arrest and criminalization. We have to carefully weigh the costs that can be inflicted on us and our communities by a state that is driven to target those who are racialized ahead of those who are white."[58] Suzanne Dhaliwal, a British climate justice and decolonial activist of color, also emphasized how the protest tactics of XR have pushed out minority-led organizations from public spaces, "It's removed even people like me who were used to doing lots of direct action from even feeling safe to do that anymore."[59]

Daze Aghaji, an XR insider of color, acknowledges the problematic nature of mass arrests, but disagrees that XR pressures everyone to get arrested, "I'm personally non-arrestable, and this is a decision that should be made by every individual. I understand that being a black woman, the police are not going to [treat me the] same as a 40-year-old white woman. So, I'm not going to put myself in that position. And within XR you're not forced to."[60] This clarification, however, reflects power blindness and exclusion. If a vulnerable XR participant had to "freely" choose against getting arrested at an XR protest, she might be perceived as not fully committed to the movement or might have to exclude herself from an important aspect of XR's core identity. Many of these fears have come true as the UK Police, Crime, Sentencing and Courts Bill (2022) gives police new powers to impose a variety of conditions on the staging of protests. Most controversially, it has made it illegal for people to occupy public spaces using the rationale of "recklessly causing public nuisance."[61]

XR's bias toward the privileged groups also spilled over into insensitivity toward the working class. In October 2019, XR activists blockaded London's underground train system at several stations. The intention was to jolt people out of their presumed apathy toward ongoing environmental and climate crises. However, the protest at the Canning Town station triggered a major backlash as disruption in the commute delayed many working-class Londoners. Protesters were dragged down from the roof of the carriage and kicked by commuters. An angry commuter shouted, "I have to get to work too—I have to feed my kids."[62] These commuters were disproportionally dependent on public transport and being late to work could have meant a quick pink slip for them.[63] XR's disruption of one of the most environment friendly modes of transport also didn't go down well with observers.

XR's blindness toward racism has been called out on multiple occasions. A 2019 tweet by XR exhorted the police and courts to let go its nonviolent protestors indulging in a noble cause, and instead focus on "knife crime," dog whistle for petty crimes stereotypically associated with youth of color. Messages such as these reflect racist stereotypes held and reproduced by the movement and make it unwelcoming for people of color. Guppy Bola, a British activist, sees it "feeding into a racist narrative."[64] BIPOC participants and allies have pressured XR to center anti-racism in its worldview. Yet, Jonathan Logan, one of XR America's founders, says, "If we don't solve climate change, Black lives don't matter. If we don't solve climate change now, LGBTQ [people] don't matter. If we don't solve climate change right now, all of us together in one big group, the #MeToo movement doesn't matter ... I can't say it hard enough. We don't have time to argue about social justice."[65] This dominant XR strategy assumes that focusing on questions of gender and racial justice will drive potential supporters away and undermine climate action.

XR-UK and XR-Global also reflect this self-imagination of being "beyond politics." A 2021 blog post from XR-Global explains its third demand, "Go Beyond Politics," as the need for Citizen's Assembly as the source of national decision-making.[66] Albeit XR-UK has reframed the third demand slightly: "If we are to have any hope of coping with the emergency, we have to move beyond the politics that have so far held us back." While these descriptions suggest a narrow meaning for the term political, minority activists still find them problematic. Guppy Bola, from Wretched of the Earth, emphasizes how the apparent threats of "mass climate migrations" can attract the xenophobic political right toward XR, further endangering the prospects for immigrant participation in climate movements.[67]

The Tensions and Tribulations within Youth Climate Movements

XR and FFF have sparked widespread enthusiasm about the promises of global youth climate activism. Their nonviolent nature and innovative styles of protest have attracted significant media attention. Tech-savvy young participants routinely leverage social media for information sharing, publicity, and recruitment of supporters resulting in hundreds of international chapters and affiliate organizations. These movements have gained the attention of not only youth but also grownups across the globe. However, as many climate justice activists have argued, these movements must also address several limitations.

Both movements rely heavily on science, assuming it to be a neutral catalyst for transformative change, despite the history of science being steeped in Eurocentrism and colonialism. Treating science as neutral creates the real possibility of vested interests hijacking science to serve vested interests. For example, analysis of more than 900 diplomatic cables revealed that American diplomats had lobbied aggressively to promote GM food crops such as soybeans in Europe and other countries.[68] The contrast between the generally strict GMO regulations in Europe versus the lax regulations in the United States offers useful insights about the contingent nature of science-society-policy interface.[69] We also discussed in Chapter 3 how vested interests attached to specific climate technologies are pushing for dangerous planet altering solutions. While these youth movements cite science as the basis for the Paris Agreement's goals of emission reduction, we know that these targets are not enough, enforceable, or just. The Paris goal of holding the *average* global atmospheric temperature increase below 2°C signals tolerating regional temperature increases of up to 4°C, especially in the mid-latitude tropics, which will hurt populations that contribute the least to climate change.[70]

FFF and XR emerged in Europe and remained Eurocentric for a considerable time before their expansion brought in activists and members of color. Both have been accused of racism within their organizational structures where representation and leadership are skewed toward European activists. These tensions are linked to the efforts, especially within the XR, to fashion "apolitical" or "beyond political" identities to create a Big-Tent approach inclusive of the beliefs of potential supporters from across the socio-political spectrum. For example, while right-wing critics have labeled XR as "middle-class layabouts or drug-addled hippies, dangerous killjoys or extremist anarchists," XR has avoided confronting them or conservative groups, and parties.[71] This is not only a refusal to acknowledge the complexity of the climate crisis but is also likely shortsighted for the future growth of these movements.

BIPOC communities overwhelmingly support environmental movements and climate action, in stark contrast to affluent white communities whose structural advantages insulate them from climate change.[72] Being apolitical therefore is neither good for confronting the root causes of the climate crises, nor is it a sound recruitment strategy.[73] Yet, most influential climate activists in the Global North continue to promote a Eurocentric perspective on climate, science, and society. They tend to assume a monolithic view of "humanity" as if we are all in the same boat. Such stances constitute a denial of the differences of race, caste, class, gender, and other forms of privileges between and within nations. Such naïve assumptions blur the distinction between the small but affluent, hyper-consuming populations with enormous carbon footprints, and the masses who are extremely resource poor and yet the primary victims of climate change. The stunted growth of FFF and XR in Asia, Africa, and Latin America illustrates the limited relevance of their North Atlantic visions and strategies.

We have detailed these limitations with a sincere hope that these two movements can truly transform. In the next section, we discuss some of the changes that have indeed been triggered by demands and pushbacks made by insiders and outsiders in both movements, often BIPOC members and supporters.

Youthful Rays of Hope in Western Climate Movements

The limitations we outlined above notwithstanding, the most encouraging element of XR and FFF is that they do not individualize the responsibility for addressing climate change. Instead of focusing on individualistic acts like green consumption or littering, both movements emphasize collective mobilization and have attracted large followings among youth in the Global North. Of late, these movements have also promised to listen to criticism, reflect on it, and to change to be more inclusive and just. These shifts have been pushed from both within and outside their organizations.

XR has undergone introspection after fierce pushbacks by dissenting members, allies, critics, and the community at large. Kofi Mawuli Klu, a senior insider and spokesperson for XR's Internationalist Solidarity network, acknowledged the shortcomings of XR's planning that led to the disruption of working-class Londoners' daily commute. He asked for patience as XR has actively listened to activists like himself and has agreed to bring about changes.[74] XR Youth, a new campaign that branched out from XR, has shaped up as a more diverse movement sharply focused on the Global South and Indigenous communities. Priyamvada Gopal, a University of Cambridge Don, echoes this hope, "My sense is also that because it is a growing movement that is bringing different kinds of people on board, particularly younger people, important discussions around race and geopolitics are starting to happen and that is welcome."[75]

In July 2020, XR apologized for being insensitive to the challenges that mass arrests pose for protestors of color, "We recognize now that our tactic of arrest has made it easier for people of privilege to participate and that our behaviors and attitudes fed into the system of white supremacy. We're sorry this recognition comes so late." XR also clarified their view of the police and their past collaborations with officers in facilitating arrests, "We view the police as professionals who may or may not act with integrity, and who represent an organization that is institutionally racist—not as allies. We do not negotiate with them, speak with them about organizers, or name people involved in protests. Nor do we feel awarding gifts and chanting *We love you* to the police is appropriate."[76] The apology was accompanied by a list of specific actions that XR-UK has decided to take in order to prioritize anti-racism. This includes establishing and funding a dedicated internal group, XR-International Solidarity Network (XRISN), to support XR groups in the Global South.[77] Perhaps most importantly, in November 2020, XR-UK distanced itself from Roger Hallam, one of its key founders. In doing this, XR also cited the role that Roger Hallam played in setting up XR America, which rejects the need for addressing questions of social and racial justice as crucial ingredients in the broader climate movement. These remarkable changes in XR and FFF have reaffirmed hopes about their future role in meaningful environmental actions.

FFF's socio-technical vision for the future, for example, is now split because of debates between two groups with diverse visions. One of these groups relies on an apolitical form of science and demands pragmatic reforms that adhere to the Paris goals. The other faction, mainly BIPOC individuals and groups, has called out such demands as too technology-centric, and not radical enough to bring about systemic change. While Greta Thunberg personally acknowledges issues of justice, equity, and need for systemic change, FFF as a movement did not formally center them in its key demands. Speaking at the 2018 COP24, Greta asserted, "Our biosphere is being sacrificed so that rich people in countries like mine can live in luxury. It is the sufferings of the many which pay for the luxuries of the few," and "we need to focus on equity. And if solutions within the system are so impossible to find, maybe we should change the system itself."[78]

These internal debates have led to specific changes within FFF. "Ensure climate justice and equity" now appears as the second main demand on FFF's website:[79] FFF's USA chapter now includes demands such as "invest in social justice movements that decolonize …" and "combat colonialist and imperialist ideology and hold wealthy former colonial powers accountable for perpetrating destruction." These shifts signal the movement's willingness to engage with systemic racism and international inequalities.

FFF's X/Twitter postings also disseminate information about the struggles of minority groups across the globe facing internal colonialism. For example, FFF tweeted in solidarity with colonized Palestinian people in 2021, "We stand with the Palestinian people against settler-colonization. We stand against all forms of colonialism and systematic repression by militaries and institutions."[80] In April

2022, FFF tweeted in support of the Baloch ethnic minority in Pakistan that has been brutalized by the military for decades while the state has mined copper and gold in the Balochistan province.[81] FFF India has been tweeting its support for Indigenous activists in Chattisgarh province resisting coal mining in their homeland and forests.[82] In another sign of these new commitments, FFF India started a petition to free jailed Indigenous rights defender Hidme Markam, who has been fighting state violence aimed at the takeover of tribal land for corporate interests.[83] These engagements suggest an inclusive and intersectional turn within FFF. Credit goes to the ethical stand, commitments, courage, and actions of BIPOC activists from within and other environmental and climate justice movements. It is important to be aware of many such activists and their struggles grounded in their life experiences from across the world.

Young Black activist Mari Copney, better known as Little Miss Flint, has been advocating for clean water for children and local communities in Flint, Michigan. Ugandan activist Vanessa Nakate has been an advocate for endangered forests in Congo and a founder of the Rise Up Africa movement that seeks to amplify the voice of African activists. Kevin Patel, an American teenager from Los Angeles, drew inspiration from his own health problems caused by air pollution to launch an intersectional youth group to advocate for the rights of marginalized youth and climate justice. Autumn Peltier, an Indigenous Canadian activist, has been a water warrior since she was eight years old. Tonny Nowshin, a Bangladesh-born German climate justice activist, organized a campaign to save the world's largest mangrove forests—Sunderban—from state-sponsored coal mining. Indian climate activist Disha Ravi, one of the founders of Fridays for Future India, was arrested in 2021 for supporting Indian farmers' protests. Jamie Sarai Margolin, a Jewish-Queer-Latina activist with Colombian heritage, founded the Zero Hour campaign for the rights of Indigenous communities and bio-diversity conservation. Sophie

Figure 9 Filipino climate justice activist of Youth Advocates for climate action Philippines Mitzi Jonelle Tan (R) and Indian climate justice activist of Fridays for future India Disha Ravi (L) during a photo session in Paris on June 20, 2023.

Photo by JOEL SAGET/AFP/Getty Images

"I also realised, during my time in custody, that most people knew little or nothing about climate activism or climate justice. My grandparents, who are farmers, indirectly birthed my climate activism. I had to bear witness to how the water crisis affected them, but my work was reduced to tree plantation drives and clean-ups which are important but not the same as struggling for survival. Climate Justice is about intersectional equity. It is about being radically inclusive of all groups of people, so that everyone has access to clean air, food and water. As a dear friend always says, 'Climate Justice isn't just for the rich and the white'. It is a fight alongside those who are displaced; whose rivers have been poisoned; whose lands were stolen; who watch their houses get washed away every other season; and those who fight tirelessly for what are basic human rights. We fight alongside those actively silenced by the masses and portrayed as 'voiceless'..."[84]

— Fridays for Future India activist Disha Ravi, who was arrested by the Delhi police in February 2021 on charges of sedition, criminal conspiracy and promoting hatred by editing and circulating a Google Docs "toolkit" in solidarity with the Indian farmers' movement.

Ming, a youth leader organizing local groups to create awareness about challenges facing Black New Yorkers, leads the Defund NYPD campaign. Ecuadorian Indigenous youth activists, Leo Cerda and Nina Gualinga, have been fighting human rights abuses in the Amazon at the hands of oil companies and other industrial groups that have displaced thousands of Indigenous families.

These and many other activists, allies, observers, and scholars have forced FFF and XR to reckon with their privileges and blind spots. It is evident that cross-fertilization, collaborations, and global solidarities are essential for the maturing and growth of diverse transnational climate movements. It is in these dynamic changes—from within and outside of the climate youth movement where we see the strongest potential for forming alliances between environmental and climate justice activists from the Global South with those fighting these battles in the Global North; for creating solidarities between communities spread across the axes of identity, class, and interests; for learning from each other, and for nurturing a truly decolonized environmentalism. These emergent solidarities are also valuable because repression of climate activism is likely to be increasingly common, as the climate crisis worsens.[85] Deep solidarities that recognize and seek to mend social and economic inequalities among different groups of climate activists will be necessary for safeguarding climate activism, especially in the Global South.

In the concluding chapter, we discuss diverse inspirational movements, campaigns, and perspectives and draw lessons from their struggles, visions, and strategies that can provide us with the building blocks of a decolonized environmentalism.

Forging Solidarities for Emancipatory and Regenerative Environmentalisms

Catastrophic wildfires in Australia, the Western United States, and the Amazon, massive loss of biodiversity, record-breaking temperatures throughout the year, and disruption of seasons have brought environmental consciousness to the center of media and popular culture. While Amitav Ghosh is nudging the literary world to engage with this changed world in their work, newspapers such as the *Guardian* have adopted new vocabulary to acknowledge that we are in the midst of a climate crisis. If it is already not, environmentalism is set to be the "ism" of our age. Yet, as we have argued in this book, mainstream environmentalism is entrenched in the problematic ideologies of European modernity, colonialism, and capitalism. This environmentalism is not just exclusionary and unjust, it is also ineffective.

Environmentalism needs a radical reset if we want to protect the integrity of planetary systems and the lives of human and nonhuman species. The increasingly vocal demands for decolonizing environmentalism are yet to translate into new environmental policies, programs, and strategies. In this book, we have sought to make a bridge by explaining how colonial histories and capitalist ideologies are embedded within and continue to shape Euro-American environmentalism. In this chapter, we outline the key building blocks and pathways for decolonizing environmentalism. To us, it is not just about reinterpreting environmentalism from a "non-Western" lens or putting more women, Queer, and BIPOC members on governing boards of environmental organizations. While greater representation of those who have been excluded from environmental organizations and movements is necessary, it is not sufficient to decolonize environmentalism. The goal instead should be to purge mainstream environmentalism of its foundational conceptual problems by developing a new praxis that brings together the intellectual and material dimensions of a decolonial environmentalism. In developing this approach, we take on the intellectual challenge that "Decolonization is not a Metaphor."[1]

Before diving deeper into the core arguments of this chapter, let us collect the key insights we have discussed so far. We began by problematizing popular individualistic actions such as responsible consumption, fair trade, and de-littering. Corporations have exploited this mundane environmentalism of conscious consumers by using it as a green façade that hides environmental destruction caused by extractive industries. Mundane environmentalism goes hand in hand with heroic environmentalism led by celebrities from the Global North. These celebrity environmentalists fly to remote corners of the world, often by private jets, to save endangered species and "pristine nature" from "natives." The mutually reinforcing nexus of mundane and heroic environmentalisms undercuts collective action for the environment, and accords legitimacy to the spurious belief that individual actions alone can avert environmental destruction.

The failures of mainstream environmentalism—in mitigating deforestation, biodiversity loss, declining pollinators, loss of seeds, or the climate crisis—have not led to any fundamental rethink. This is because the most devastating consequences of environmental loss are experienced by Indigenous Peoples, racial minorities, communities of color, and working-class people, who are excluded from mainstream environmentalism. Some of the most popular policies and programs for protecting the environment are designed to preserve the privileges of the elite. Environmental action continues to be premised on a colonial mindset that assumes Indigenous and rural communities to be incapable of stewarding the environment. Powerful multilateral agencies such as the World Bank, IMF, and WTO work with domestic elites to impose extractive projects justified in the name of economic development, which perpetuates internal colonialism.

Growing cacophony around solar geoengineering raises a new specter of unprecedented planetary risks. Untested technologies such as solar radiation management have become buzzwords in climate change circles. Unlike immersive virtual reality games where players can walk out unscathed once they are bored, these technologies have real and serious risks. They can upend hydrological cycles and monsoons in the tropics where the vast majority of the human population resides. The euphoria around these dangerous technologies—promoted aggressively by a group of physicists, policy think tanks, business elites, and corporate philanthropists—reflects Eurocentric modernity and the masculine impulse to control and conquer nature. Simultaneously, there is growing doublespeak about respecting Indigenous rights in global conservation and environmental policymaking. Loud pledges respecting Indigenous rights are used to deflect attention from blatant denials of autonomy, agency, and sovereignty of Indigenous and peasant communities who are frequently dispossessed and displaced in the name of conservation. Such domination notwithstanding, resistance has grown.

Myriad global, regional, and national movements have sparked hope in the last few years. Fridays for Futures (FFF), and Extinction Rebellion (XR)—two movements we discussed previously—mobilize citizens to demand that governments act on climate change. On the other hand, the Fossil Fuel Divestment movement, which we discuss in this chapter, targets private investments into and public subsidies for fossil fuel corporations. Despite their European origins, both FFF and XR movements have borrowed tactics from a much longer history of collective mobilization and people's initiatives from across the world. This includes strikes, civil disobedience, and mass arrests to exhort world leaders to listen to the scientific evidence on the severity of climate crisis. Their narrow focus on Western science means, however, that they fail to critically scrutinize, let alone resist, the corporate appropriation of "nature-based solutions."

In *The Nutmeg's Curse*, Amitav Ghosh reminds us that "climate change is but one aspect of a much broader planetary crisis."[2] Our current planetary crisis is a product of extractivism, exploitation of humans and nonhuman species, global inequalities, and the decimation of biodiversity in the pursuit of short-term material benefits that are concentrated in the hands of a few elites. None of these outcomes can be explained away as "unintended consequences" of capitalism. Instead, they are the core features of capitalism. This means that effective environmental and climate action cannot succeed unless the exploitative and extractive structures of neocolonial capitalism are transformed radically.[3] A decolonized environmentalism is essential for addressing global environmental and climate crises, while also addressing the conjoined crises of social, political, and economic inequalities. In the following sections, we draw inspiration and insights from ecofeminism and Black feminism and identify strategies developed by select social movements to build broad-based solidarities in pursuit of emancipatory alternatives to the status quo. These are the building blocks that we hope can be used to decolonize environmentalism.

Intellectual Foundations: Ecofeminism and Black Feminism

Ecofeminism, a philosophy that took shape in the 1970s, is based on the insight that gendered social norms of patriarchal social and economic systems lead to unjust dominance over women and nature.[4]

By implication, ecofeminists envision the liberation of women and nature to be inherently intertwined with one another. In the first few decades of its evolution, the dominant strands of ecofeminism reflected the concerns of white women scholars and activists. They claimed to value and learn from Indigenous women's environmental wisdom and commitment, yet in most cases, these efforts led to the simplification and misappropriation of Indigenous wisdom.

Ecofeminist critiques of mainstream environmental scholarship took two paths. The first, cultural ecofeminism, focuses on the *gendered* nature of everyday practices at an interpersonal level. Based on simplistic comparisons of women and nature, adherents of this popular approach celebrate spiritual connections between nature and womanhood to inspire responsible consumption. A single-minded emphasis on *interpersonal* gendered inequalities distracts from confronting the structural inequalities of capitalism, which is at the root of current environmental and climate crises.[5] On the contrary, associating private ownership and consumption of goods with women's empowerment or demanding that nature and care economy be valued within the market system gives in to the logic of capitalism.[6]

The second path, radical ecofeminism, emphasizes the material aspects of nature-society relations and the role of social structures, class, and power.[7] Maria Miles and Vandana Shiva's early Marxist feminist work centered global capitalism in their analysis of biodiversity loss, environmental crisis, dispossession, and food crisis across the globe.[8] However, these early articulations of ecofeminism mainly reflected elite perspectives, often at the cost of the views of marginalized groups. For example, Vandana Shiva, the face of ecofeminism from the Global South, universalizes the experience of upper-caste Hindu women from rural North India over all women.[9] Shiva's ecofeminism obscures the violent structures of caste and social hierarchy that shape the struggles of all women, especially, Dalit and Indigenous women.[10] Shiva's uncritical promotion of vegetarianism is blind to its ideological nature in India, where vegetarianism is used to perpetuate caste- and religion-based hierarchies and to marginalize omnivorous communities, especially Dalits and Muslims.[11] Despite these problems, such elitist versions of ecofeminism gained popularity among environmentally conscious people in the Global North.

A similar case of depoliticizing radical ideas can be seen in the celebration of Nobel Laureate Wangari Mathai's work. The Norwegian Nobel Committee recognized Maathai's contribution to "sustainable development, democracy and peace," commending her struggles against "political oppression," her contributions to "the fight for democratic rights," and especially for helping Kenyan "women to better their situation."[12] However, popular environmental media emphasizes "tree-planting" campaigns as her main contribution. Her obituary on the UN website headlined her as "the woman of trees."[13] Several popular books convey the same docile versions of her work: *Wangari Maathai: The Woman Who Planted a Million Trees*; *Mama Miti: Wangari Maathai, and the Trees of Kenya*; and *Seeds of Change: Planting a Path to Peace*. Reducing Maathai's work to the act of tree plantation is reminiscent of individualization of Rachel Carson's environmentalism. It also reflects the tendencies within mainstream environmentalism to valorize tree-planting as an individual heroic environmental action. Ecofeminist analyses of Maathai's work celebrate her radical contributions to resist "environmental and political oppression, empowering rural women, and to enact a political consciousness toward democracy and environmental justice."[14] Mathai and other feminist activists of color have contributed intersectional praxis in ecofeminism, which should be a core element in decolonized environmentalism.[15]

Considering that intersectionality can be applied in a variety of ways, it is important to clarify a fundamental and frequently occurring confusion about intersectional ecofeminism. Early ecofeminism reflected intersectional thinking to identify the coproduction of "the oppressions of women, animals, and the environment ... [yet it viewed] women as one undifferentiated group."[16] A deeper form of intersectional ecofeminism requires mapping the insidious conflation of nature, race, ethnicity, and women. Popular culture portrays women as "naturally caring," Indigenous People as one with nature, and Black people as wild and unruly, while trying to contain "pristine nature" in enclaves of national parks and nature reserves.[17] Each of these stereotypes reinforces the power of dominant actors and frames and contributes to the perpetuation of the status quo. Making a distinction between "ordinary" and pristine nature and locking pristine nature away in the safe boxes of nature reserves enables commodification and merchandizing of nature.[18] Our approach to intersectional ecofeminism shuns monolithic categorization in favor of developing a comprehensive understanding of the systemic oppression against nature, women, Indigenous Peoples, Black, and other marginalized communities. To do this, it is important to pursue a deeper engagement with Black feminist writings on nature, which do not always use the label of ecofeminism.

Black queer feminist activist, scholar, and teacher bell hooks remind us that over 90 percent of Black folk in post-emancipation America came from agrarian backgrounds where they were farm workers and sharecroppers invested in local food production. In hooks' childhood in rural Kentucky, being close to nature meant being free and beyond oppressive social structures. Her family later moved to a city where they lived on the margins of the white world that they entered to serve others and from where they returned to the dilapidated Black neighborhood across the railway tracks.[19] Millions of Black Americans fleeing Jim Crow laws undertook the Great Migration to cities in the North in search of jobs and better lives. Alienation from nature in the rural South and new forms of segregation in the Northern cities created new traumas that, according to hooks, can only be addressed by re-forging regenerative relations with nature.[20] Black and Indigenous self-recovery is intimately tied to the nurturing role of ecology while also confronting the systems that simultaneously dislocate and oppress nature and marginalized people.

The potential for such a broad-based recovery and regeneration is inhibited by the tendency on part of some environmentalists to create a false equivalence between, say, subsistence use of nature and industrial-scale mining. hooks offered a nuanced and situated perspective based on her lived experiences in which coal was mined for subsistence, for indoor heating during the cold winters. Nature-based subsistence creates a respectful relationship with nature, which is often disrupted by industrial extractivism. Mining of coal through "mountain top removal" techniques decimated Appalachia's socio-ecological systems and rendered thousands of coal miners jobless. The logic of Racial Capitalism soon framed these dislocated workers— White and Black alike—as "Hillbillies." hooks argues that the popular myth of the Hillbilly is nothing but a pejorative backlash against those who resisted capitalism; popular culture portrays them as unworthy of social acceptance and respect.[21]

hooks and other intersectional feminist scholars offer a solidaristic view of marginalized and exploited people cutting across the boundaries of gender and race. As such, they build on insights from Black Socialist Feminist groups, such as the Combahee River Collective. Members of the collective argued that Black women's position at the bottom of social and economic hierarchies meant that their liberation would demand "the destruction of all the systems of oppression."[22] Yet, bringing about such transformation requires mass mobilization and political action, as demonstrated by resistance movements of people of color, Indigenous groups, women, Queer folks, and youth groups. We now turn to four such movements, which offer deep insights about scaling up grassroots mobilization for transformative changes in the larger structures of power and privilege.

Figure 10 Climate Justice March London. Climate justice campaigners march from the Shell Centre to Trafalgar Square to demand urgent climate finance and reparations for loss and damage for Global South communities on November 12, 2022, in London, United Kingdom. The march was part of a Global Day of Action called by African climate campaign groups at COP27.

Photo by Mark Kerrison/In Pictures / Getty Images.

Inspirational Social Movements

Philosophers and thinkers help us envision a new world that is sometimes difficult to see from our current standpoints. Yet as Brazilian educator-philosopher Paulo Freire argued, "knowledge emerges only through invention and re-invention, through the restless, impatient, continuing, hopeful inquiry human beings pursue in the world, with the world, and with each other."[23] As such, both the task of building emancipatory philosophies and translating them into mass movements require a serious engagement with social movements. We will now take you on a truly global tour to showcase four contemporary social movements that have served as an inspiration for this work. These movements and the praxis they have developed make visible the main elements of an insurgent, transformative, and decolonized environmentalism. We start with Black Lives Matter, which is tied, somewhat counter-intuitively, to the efforts to decolonize environmentalism.

Black Lives Matter

Black Lives Matter (BLM) was born with a 2013 Facebook post by Oakland-based labor organizer Alicia Garza, after a white man was acquitted in the murder of an African American teenager Trayvon Martin. Soon, the hashtag #BlackLivesMatter spread from Facebook, Twitter, Instagram, and other social media spaces to large-scale mobilization on the streets. Another round of protests started after the police killing of Michael Brown in Ferguson, Missouri, in 2014, and spread globally in the summer of 2020 after the murder of George Floyd by a Minnesota police officer. A decentralized coalition of over a hundred local and international BLM chapters led these protests. It attracted 15–26 million protestors in the United States, making it one of the largest movements in the country's history.[24] BLM has fostered a global conversation about the impact of state violence on Black and other communities of color, driven critical dialogues on transforming American democracy, and put tremendous pressure on institutions of state and society to end discrimination against Black communities.[25]

BLM also has strong links with environmental and climate justice. Environmental Justice scholars Lindsey Dillon and Julie Sze see the last words of George Floyd "I can't breathe" as an embodiment of the precarity of Black lives. It points to the social "conditions through which breath is constricted or denied."[26] BLM's demands resonated with several environmental and climate justice movements. For example, the Central Coast Climate Justice Network (C3JN) affirmed, "There is no climate justice without racial justice."[27]

BLM's demands also echo the insightful interventions that Ambassador Lumumba Di-Aping, the lead negotiator of the G77 group of 130 low- and middle-income countries, made at the global climate negotiations at Copenhagen in December 2009. He argued that a 2°C target would lead parts of tropical Africa to heat up between 3°C and 4°C, a catastrophic scenario which would sacrifice millions of African lives. Lumumba called the Copenhagen Pact "a suicide pact, an incineration pact in order to maintain the economic dominance of a few countries."[28] Lumumba's interventions inspired UK activist and decolonization scholar Leon Sealey-Huggins to argue that global climate policy regime is structured in ways that "devalue Black life."[29]

Today, as we stare at the prospect of an above 3°C heating of the planet, [the global climate justice movement] climate activists would do well to build on the message of valuing Black people's lives.[30] This is especially so because Black communities and other marginalized groups are the main victims of a fossil-fuel-driven extractive capitalism. Thankfully, the youth-led Fossil Fuel Divestment (FFD) movement has focused on confronting and undermining the fossil fuel industry. We now turn to FFD for insights about broadening and deepening the impact of the global climate movement.

Fossil Free Movement and Youth Climate Movements

The Fossil Fuel Divestment (FFD) movement is a student-led movement inspired from the global divestment movement against South African apartheid. Their modest campaign started in 2011 at Swarthmore College where they pressured the college to divest from fossil fuels. In April 2014, Nobel peace laureate Desmond Tutu, one of the prominent figures in the struggle for South Africa's liberation, gave a shout-out to the nascent FFD movement. Writing in the British daily *The Guardian*, he said:

People of conscience need to break their ties with corporations financing the injustice of climate change. We can, for instance, boycott events, sports teams and media programming sponsored by fossil-fuel energy companies. We can demand that the advertisements of energy companies carry health warnings ... we can take steps to reduce its political clout, and hold those who rake in the profits accountable for cleaning up the mess.[31]

In a decade since then, the FFD has gained support not only of institutions of higher education but also from numerous faith-based institutions, philanthropic foundations, healthcare organizations, governments, cities, pension funds, NGOs, and even profit-making corporations. As of January 2024, FFD has garnered divestment commitments worth $40.63 trillion from 1,613 institutions worldwide.[32] The impact of FFD appears to be more pronounced in countries with relatively more stringent environmental policy regimes and less effective in countries that heavily subsidize the fossil fuel industry.[33] Notwithstanding the variable results of FFD's divestment work, it has successfully shaken the moral license that the fossil fuel industry enjoyed as the harbinger of modernity.[34]

The FFD movement has sought to transform climate action into the leading moral issue of this generation. To these ends, the FFD has combined the aggregation and packaging of scientific facts, with potent moral arguments that it disseminates via local and international campaigning, direct action, and lobbying aimed at influencing institutional investors.[35] In addition to calling into question its moral and social license, FFD campaign aims to stop all new fossil fuel projects with the goal of "the ultimate demise of the industry."[36] There are some signs that these strategies are beginning to make an impact. Morgan Stanley, for example, has been advising investors since 2016 to adopt strategies that reduce or eliminate investing in fossil fuels.[37] In a 2017 strategic report, the oil major Shell acknowledged the potential impact of FFD campaigns: "Some groups are pressuring certain investors to divest their investments in fossil fuel companies ... [which] could have a material adverse effect on the price of our securities and our ability to access equity capital markets."[38]

FFD campaign's focus on the moral dimension of climate crisis resonates strongly with Black Lives Matter activists, many institutional investors, and global leaders such as Desmond Tutu. FFD's demands have also been adopted by other social movements. The Movement for Black Lives (M4BL), a space for Black organizations across the United States, called for "divestment from exploitative forces," including industrial multinational use of fossil fuels, which should be used for new investment in community-based sustainable energy solutions.[39] These cross-cutting solidarities reverberated in the public domain after the oil giant Chevron tweeted in support of "black lives matter" in June 2020: "Racism has no place in America ... we stand in support of the black community and all those seeking systematic change." Communities for a Better Environment, a California-based environmental justice organization, responded: "Your performative solidarity with the Black community is an absolute joke ... You should be ashamed of yourself for killing, poisoning and ruining the health and lives of Black people all over the world."[40]

Overall, FFD has reframed the climate debate as a "political question in a way that directly challenges the post-political assumptions" of climate change as a techno-managerial subject.[41] It has also trained an impressive cohort of activists who are at the forefront of both the Sunrise Movement and the Green New Deal in the United States.[42] The other two youth climate movements we discussed in Chapter 6 have also been broadening their strategies. FFF stands strongly with Indigenous Peoples' movements, including against the imposition of renewable energy infrastructure in their territories. XR too is undergoing major changes, both within the movement and in its strategies for mobilizing the public.

Global, national, and local climate movements have an opportunity to learn from these experiences to build strong bridges with several long-standing social and environmental justice movements in different parts of the world. Building such solidarities requires grounding these disparate movements in longer histories of settler colonialism, land ownership, corporate land and sea grabs, and resistance from people's movements devoted to protecting local livelihoods.[43] Toward this end, we discuss an inspirational movement centered on agroecology and peasant livelihoods that has grown from its grassroots beginnings to foster a global movement advocating for regenerative agroecology and food sovereignty.

The La Via Campesina Movement for Food Sovereignty

As this book goes to the press, the UN Secretary-General Antonio Guterres warns that "climate disasters imperil food production," urging the UN Security Council to address the impact of food shortages and rising temperatures on international peace and security. Mr. Guterres is right to be concerned about the current security situation in Ukraine and Gaza, widespread hunger in other world regions affected by civil and political conflicts, and that the climate crisis is further worsening the situation. However, each of these outcomes is owed to trigger-happy politicians and a profit-hungry defense industry that is exacerbating the climate crisis. Our security crisis has absolutely no relationship whatsoever with Mr. Guterres' misplaced quip that "empty bellies fuel unrest."[44] Instead, the climate securitization narrative, which informs the UN chief's comments, is often used to promote corporate control over global food supplies on the pretext of ameliorating hunger and to seek increased public funding for security agencies.[45] We can do better than weaponizing hunger.

A global community of activists, scholars, and legal experts have developed a redemptive alternative to the global food question. We are referring to the global food sovereignty movement led by La Via

Campesina (LVC). Peasant representatives, including women, men, and people of diverse identities and ethnicities, affiliated with small-scale food cooperatives and farmers organizations from different continents, founded La Via Campesina in 1993 at a meeting in Mons, Belgium. LVC has its headquarters in Paris, though its leadership rotates between different regional chapters. Starting as a grassroots movement, LVC has spearheaded the development and enactment of the United Nations Declaration on the Rights of Peasants and Other People Working in Rural Areas (UNDROP) in October 2018. LVC's path has been full of challenges and its strategies far from perfect. This is why its multi-faceted success offers four precious lessons for building a movement to decolonize the environment.

The first lesson relates to the importance of praxis-based movement building. LVC demands a structural transformation derived from the practices of agroecology and food sovereignty. Agroecology is a holistic system that applies "ecological concepts, principles and knowledge to agricultural production rather than relying on external toxic inputs" like fertilizers, pesticides, and herbicides.[46] The broader food sovereignty movement stands for the rights of peasants, family-based small farms, migrant workers, as well as community rights over land, water, forests, fisheries, and seeds. LVC's model of multilevel action and advocacy for agroecological food sovereignty is designed to respond to the goals of securing community control over agriculture and food production.

The second main insight is related to how LVC has operationalized intersectionality. The LVC-led food sovereignty movement's deep engagement with women farmers and farmers of color (who form the majority of the global peasant population) places it at the intersection of gender, race, and class. Noticeably, women farmer leaders waged decades-long struggles, including by creating and strengthening the autonomous women's organization and associated political spaces within LVC. These spaces proved to be crucial for building women's political autonomy and collective capacity to challenge patriarchal privilege, and "radicalizing food sovereignty with a feminist perspective."[47] The third valuable insight focuses on the framing of LVC's identity as a transnational peasant movement, which demands a multi-scalar approach to movement building. LVC draws on insights from "Campesino a Campesino" (peasant to peasant) peer learning networks on the practice of agroecology. These horizontal networks have their roots in the mobilization of peasants in Nicaragua, Guatemala, Cuba, and Mexico resisting both US and Soviet imperialism, while experimenting with agroecological practices locally, and sharing knowledge and skills with each other.[48] Campesino a Campesino networks constitute an important foundation for LVC's advocacy of agroecology and food sovereignty, including in various forums at the United Nations. These strategies have been central to LVC's efforts to resist the forces of Global Capitalism, which has both the peasant and the countryside in its crosshair.[49]

The fourth insight from LVC's work pertains to its success in bridging distinct struggles unfolding simultaneously at local and global scales. The most shining example of that success is its contribution to the adoption of UNDROP, which offers the strongest available measures against the ongoing processes of corporate land grabs, including green grab that has been justified in the name of nature conservation or climate mitigation. These successes of the LVC show that the forces of globalization can be harnessed toward emancipatory politics. In contrast to transnational corporations, which are controlled by entities in the Global North, LVC chapters represent vulnerable regions both in the Global North and in the Global South.[50] It is present in eighty-one countries across nine global regions with each region represented by one woman and one man elected to its transnational decision-making body. Moreover, instead of building a monolithic global movement, it also collaborates with autonomous regional movements, such as the Alliance for Food Sovereignty in Africa (AFSA).[51]

Figure 11 Delegates from more than 40 countries representing social movements, unions, and communities affected by human rights violations by transnational companies met in Geneva in October 2018 at the fourth session of The Intergovernmental Working Group on Transnational Corporations and Other Business Enterprises. These activists developed an international legally binding human rights law instrument to regulate the activities of transnational corporations and other business enterprises.

Photo by Victor Barro / Friends of the Earth

It would be a mistake to romanticize LVC as it remains a work in progress. Its expansive scale of operation has led to a great deal of diversity of approaches and motivations among its constituent regional and national chapters.[52] It continues to engage across the class divide between peasants and medium to large landholders who may not share LVC's agenda of supporting migrant workers and subsistence farmers.[53] LVC also had some unusual advantages. Latin

America has an enviable history of labor and peasant mobilization, progressive land reforms, collective farming, and communal ownership of forestlands that helped birth the LVC. The absence of such conducive factors in other areas makes its replication difficult.[54] Yet, its imperfections make it a model worth learning from. Even as it continues to democratize from within, LVC has honed its skills in multilateral advocacy. In collaboration with other transnational advocacy groups and scholar activists, LVC has developed "a complex action repertoire" to engage with and take advantage of divisions within powerful intergovernmental institutions, including by "'naming and shaming' to isolate adversaries and collaborating with allies for mutually reinforcing benefits."[55] Two veterans of transnational food sovereignty movement have referred to them as "critical collaboration tactics," which work best when combined with strong mobilization of supporters outside the formal multilateral arena.[56]

The success of LVC and other local and transnational food movements has also made food sovereignty a target of appropriation by multinational agribusiness corporations, who often ridiculed the concept of agroecology in the past. They now seek to repackage corporatized and mechanized forms of agroecology in the garb of "climate smart agriculture" in the same way that corporations have appropriated sustainability.[57] In the face of these challenges, LVC has strongly defended its advocacy of food sovereignty, arguing that an industrialized version of agroecology is unacceptable. LVC continues to hold on to its ambition of being a politically subversive movement that resists neocolonialism, industrialism, and corporate control of agriculture and food.

Perseverance in the face of resistance from the beneficiaries of the status quo would be an integral component of any effort to bring about transformative change. There can be no better source of wisdom on longue durée of transformative changes than Indigenous Peoples. The lessons from Indigenous movements must be the biggest source of inspiration and insights for decolonizing environmentalism.

Indigenous Resistance in the Face of Climate Crisis

Indigenous Peoples and territories have been at the receiving end of the trio of colonialism, imperialism, and capitalism. The lands, waters, fisheries, and wildlife that Indigenous Peoples had stewarded for centuries became the first victims of colonial resource grabs. An estimated 8 million bison lived in the United States in 1870, but fewer than 500 of this iconic keystone species survived the colonial onslaught, leaving behind long-lasting legacies of economic precarity, loss, and mourning among Indigenous Nations and Peoples.[58] This purposeful mass slaughter of North American bison helped establish European settler colonialism—it meant commercial gains for the colonizers while also depriving Indigenous People of a crucial source of physical nourishment and spiritual strength.

The framework of environmental justice (EJ), which we discussed in Chapter 2, captures some of the long-lasting legacies of settler colonial capitalist states. EJ scholars have shown that racial minorities and other marginalized groups, including Indigenous Nations, bear a disproportionate share of the burdens of environmental pollution, testing of nuclear and other types of weapons, and disposal of toxic effluents and waste.[59] Indigenous scholars and activists have expanded EJ arguments and analysis by going beyond the frames of "race," or "environmental racism," and a distributional approach to confronting environmental harms.[60] Dina Gilio-Whitaker argues for broadening the EJ framework because Indigenous Nations are not defined merely by their ethnic or racial status, but primarily by their status as politically sovereign nations, who hold treaty rights and trust responsibilities. She argues that the demands for "restoring lands to Indigenous control is … environmental justice in the most expansive sense of the term. It is a major step in redressing relationships that have not been right since first contact."[61] Accordingly, their conceptualization of EJ incorporates the inter-generational effects of settler colonialism and their demands for territorial sovereignty.

Indigenous Peoples' movements in North America and Latin America have scored major successes in forcing national governments, inter-governmental institutions, and corporations to recognize and respect Indigenous territorial sovereignty. Well-known examples include the Standing Rock Sioux Tribe's pushback against the Dakota Access Pipeline (DAPL). This mobilization garnered widespread support nationally and internationally, as evident in the coming together of dozens of movements at the Oceti Sakowin Camp, a historic gathering of Indigenous Nations.[62] The time that Representative Alexandria Ocasio-Cortez spent at the camp reportedly motivated her to envision the Green New Deal.

The resistance to DAPL was led by water protectors, as the plans for installing the pipeline beneath the Missouri River would imperil drinking water not only for the Standing Rock tribe but for farmers, ranchers, and townspeople all along the river's course.[63] A lesser-known triumph of water warriors occurred in New Brunswick, Canada, where the Texas-based firm, SWN Resources, was granted a license to explore natural gas. As the oil rigs arrived for prospecting, a diverse group of protestors led by members of the Mi'kmaq Elsipogtog First Nation and comprising of French-speaking Acadians and English-speaking white families mounted a peaceful blockade. Women water warriors from each of those groups played a major role in halting the drilling, and eventually electing a new provincial government which put an indefinite moratorium on fracking.[64]

The emergent Land Back Movement—that seeks restitution of territory to historically dispossessed Indigenous Nations—emphasizes the centrality of territorial sovereignty within the debates on environmental and climate justice.[65] These efforts reject the lip service on "inclusion" of women, people of color, and Indigenous People in environmental decision-making, which continues to be controlled by settler institutions.[66] Instead, Indigenous activists demand that climate action can be decolonized by centering the political sovereignty of Indigenous People and matching it with the transfer of stewardship over land, forests, waters, and nonhuman relatives that share Indigenous territories.[67] The resurrection of Indigenous sovereignty is essential for making decisions that are rooted in Indigenous values and aimed at fostering long-term sustenance of the living world.

For example, recent research on oyster harvesting along the Atlantic Coast of the United States shows that decision-making systems developed by Indigenous People helped stabilize oyster reefs despite fluctuations in population densities and environmental shifts.[68] This research also showed that the Georgia Bight ecosystem, well managed through native practices for over 5000 years, underwent a precipitous decline in a mere two hundred years after the displacement of Indigenous Peoples beginning in the late 1800s. As Melanie K. Yazzie and others have shown, Indigenous resistance has created "a politics of relational life" that stands in opposition to "resource extraction," and other "violent modalit(ies) of capitalism."[69] The Land Back movement in conjunction with strict regulation of big businesses involved in resource extraction on Indigenous territories can drastically improve the prospects of environmental and climate justice. Yet, our approach to such pursuits must not be transactional.

Indigenous scholar Kyle Whyte has argued that the "entwinement of colonialism, capitalism, and industrialization" has undermined the relational values of "consent, trust, accountability, and reciprocity," which are crucial for healing the people and the planet.[70] To claim sovereignty is to claim one's right to speak for oneself—for the historically marginalized groups "leading with their values, leading with their solutions and leading with their knowledge."[71] A relational perspective on sovereignty helps put it in a broader context, with the goal of repairing the loss of collective societal abilities to undertake coordinated action urgently and justly. Such a broad framing of sovereignty opens up opportunities for applying the concept at scales other than the nation-state and to processes other than legal and political control over enclosed territories signifying nation-states. These lessons have begun to appear in the popular press. Writing about Puerto Rico, an American colony, Naomi Klein refers to "multiple sovereignties" to underline the importance of a community's autonomy for managing their food, energy, and water resources.

In the aftermath of Hurricane Maria, which caused massive damage to physical infrastructure, including a collapse of power networks, gas supply, food provisions, and health facilities, Puerto Ricans mobilized to take control of their affairs. They sought "food sovereignty, liberated from dependence on imports and agribusiness giants; energy sovereignty, liberated from fossil fuels and controlled by communities, and to some extent housing, water, and education sovereignty as well."[72] The multi-pronged nature of present-day social, environmental, and climate crises requires action on all these fronts and at multiple levels—globally, nationally, and locally. A respect for Indigenous sovereignty is closely tied to the larger economic context and collective political responses to our current crises. Yet, we urge caution in exporting the North American framework of Indigenous justice to the context of Global South, especially to countries on the continents of Africa and Asia with remarkably different histories, politics, and institutional infrastructure needed for the pursuit of Indigenous autonomy.[73]

The staggering challenges that confront the humanity and our other living kin today demand that the million mutinies that dot the landscape of present-day protests be supported by political and economic transformations. It is crucial to draw on the energies and insights from emancipatory social and environmental movements we have discussed in this chapter. By way of a conclusion, we distill the insights and provocations that we believe are essential for building a powerful harmony among diverse sets of movements devoted to a decolonized environmental movement fit for the task of protecting the planet and all its inhabitants.

In Conclusion: Toward a Decolonized and Regenerative Environmentalism

The current moment of multiple intersecting crises and breakdowns signals a profound disconnect between social, political, economic, and environmental spheres. The long-cherished ideals of environmentalism and environmental stewardship can be a source of great strength at this crucial juncture. To realize this potential of environmentalism, it must be freed of the strangulating shackles of domination and oppression. This is important not just for protecting the environment but for liberating ourselves from the unfreedoms of consumerist culture. Environmental unfreedoms, we argue following Malini Ranganathan's work, are tied to a culture that binds human happiness to conspicuous consumption.[74] The essence of decolonizing environmentalism, then, is in establishing relations of trust, respect, and accountability among sovereign human and nonhuman communities. We drew on the intellectual foundations of decolonization that are well developed in scholarly literature and activist conversations. Our goal has been to offer a broad-based political roadmap for bringing decolonization to mainstream environmentalism.

The movements that we showcased in this final chapter are shining examples of people-led mobilizations with membership cutting across age, race, gender, and borders separating the Global North from the South. Our learnings suggest that contemporary movements are most successful when they cultivate intersecting solidarities across various marginalized groups; develop situated knowledge and narratives; create transnational connections; move beyond metaphors to center material transformations; and when their organizing models enable them to counter oppressive power. These movements are not prisoners of dogma or rigid ideologies. They do not pit the current domination of markets against a desire for an ideally imagined state that is presumed to work differently and serve different goals. These movements ask us not to put our faith in prefabricated solutions of any sort. They are also not content with anarchist freedoms that cannot confront the overarching institutional power of settler colonial structures that are meant to protect the privileges of a few. Instead, the emphasis is on building social and political relations that reshape how we live and how we govern societies and economies based on non-Eurocentric, non-capitalist values and life choices.[75] Realizing these gains demands flexible organizing, intelligent strategizing, and concerted engagement with political and economic institutions at relevant scales. Each of the movements we celebrated in this chapter has sought to do that, with varying levels of success.

Today's emancipatory politics transcends the trap of localism, intervening in both domestic and global politics and political institutions. Climate youth movements mobilize moral suasion to confront the most powerful corporations and industries, compelling them to recognize and respond to these popular demands. Along the way, they learn vital lessons in internal democracy and decolonization as their imperfect praxes are subject to internal debates and contestation. They craft polycentric political spaces within, even as they seek to surmount the political-economic power of incumbents. The power within the collectives is amplified through solidarities between movements discussed above. The joined-up collectives alleviate the need for "upscaling" a monolithic global movement. As such, decolonizing movements refuse to choose between individual freedoms and collective agency, an argument that is rooted in the narrow visions of Euro-American capitalist modernity. Instead, every movement aims to decolonize oppressive societal structures by addressing a specific configuration of symbolic, material, and political aspects.

These movements demonstrate that the path to decolonizing environmentalism will require looking beyond the openings created by double or triple movements against the excesses of markets.[76] In the neocolonial capitalist world of today, people's movements must confront the combined might of the states and markets that work together to promote extractive economies. The collective grassroots power of youth activists, farmers and labor unions, worker-owned cooperatives, Indigenous Nations, and transnational movements must be leveraged to influence the working of political institutions of the state and supra-national institutions such as the United Nations. These actions would target redirecting finances from polluting industries and projects to small-scale renewable energy developments, regenerative forms of agroecology, mixed-use landscape conservation, and other forms of solidarity economy enterprises.

The architecture of praxis that we envision here shuns green-parochialism because we believe that decolonizing environmentalism requires dismantling the nature-society binary. Time is ripe for accepting that humans do not exist outside the reach of nature, nor can we continue to concoct ever more powerful technologies to manipulate planetary systems. Instead, we learn from the relational praxes of Indigenous Peoples, which shows that the health of humanity is intricately tied to the well-being of all living beings and ecosystems. In this sense, crimes against nature are also crimes against humanity. A true commitment to protecting nature and securing the well-being of our non-human kins demands that we discipline rogue human actors and agencies responsible for a vast majority of environmental degradation and the ongoing climate crisis. While liberal Western institutions have rarely been proactive in enforcing the rule of law against the most powerful polluters, coalitions of people's movements, scientists, and legal experts continue to be sources of strength in these struggles. To the extent emancipatory movements retain their autonomous agency, every incremental gain advances the agenda of building an emancipatory decolonized environmentalism. This is an endeavor for our collective future. It will need all the commitment and perseverance that we can find. And in all sincerity, decolonizing environmentalism will be a work in progress.

We hope that this book helps foster reflections and debates among diverse communities of activists, practitioners, and scholar-activists, whose ideas and actions will hopefully translate into a million mutinies against the ravages of energy-intensive lifestyles promoted by powerful corporations and condoned by present-day governments on the pretext of freedom and choice. Decolonization then is about who we aspire to be, and what sort of resources, energy, and commitments we invest in making those dreams real. For us, questioning and confronting the value of consumerism, resisting the masculine urge to dominate nature, and dethroning the technological hubris about manipulating the environment are the essential ingredients for a decolonized environmentalism. Hopefully, readers will find, join, and initiate new grassroots urban agroecological initiatives, local Fossil Free campaigns, reparatory renewable energy microgrids, and a variety of other experiments that we cannot even imagine at the moment.

In the process of writing this book, we have also thought through our own biases and limitations and invite the reader to do the same. As Jean-Paul Sartre wrote in the preface to *Wretched of the Earth*, " … the settler which is in every one of us is being savagely rooted out. Let us look at ourselves, if we can bear to, and see what is becoming of us."[77] Decolonizing environmentalism is simultaneously a deeply personal and a collective political movement. The success of this movement depends on intersecting internationalist solidarities that will demand sacrifices. We hope that this book contributes to sustained reflections, shared dreams, and collective action toward shared decolonized futures.

Notes

Chapter 1

1   *Who we are* (n.d.). Kuli Kuli Foods. https://www.kulikulifoods.com/pages/about-kuli-kuli-foods

2   Benderev, C. (2014, October 11). *Millennials: We help the earth but don't call us environmentalists.* WBUR. https://www.wbur.org/npr/355163205/millennials-well-help-the-planet-but-dont-call-us-environmentalists

3   Dunaway, F. (2017, November 21). *The "Crying Indian" ad that fooled the environmental movement.* Chicago Tribune. https://www.chicagotribune.com/opinion/commentary/ct-perspec-indian-crying-environment-ads-pollution-1123-20171113-story.html

4   Plumer, B. (2006, May 22). *The origins of anti-litter campaigns.* Mother Jones. https://www.motherjones.com/politics/2006/05/origins-anti-litter-campaigns/

5   Dunaway, *The "Crying Indian" ad that fooled the environmental movement.*

6   ING International Survey (2019, November). *Circular economy: Consumers seek help.* ING THINK. https://think.ing.com/uploads/reports/IIS_Circular_Economy_report_FINAL.PDF

7   Brenan, M. (2023, April 17). *Concern about several environmental problems dips in U.S.* Gallup. https://news.gallup.com/poll/474278/concern-several-environmental-problems-dips.aspx

8   European Union (2020, March). *Eurobarometer.* https://europa.eu/eurobarometer/surveys/detail/2257

9   Most people are unaware that another Hinkley resident Roberta Walker took on the greatest burden of collecting data and popular mobilization, though she rarely gets any credit. See this: Genecov, M. (2019, January 29). *The "Erin Brockovich" town is still toxic (and nearly*

abandoned). Grist. https://grist.org/science/the-true-story-of-the-town-behind-erin-brockovich/

10   The Editors (1999, September 15). *Rachel Carson*. Encyclopedia Britannica. https://www.britannica.com/biography/Rachel-Carson

11   Lepore, J. (2018, March 19). *The right way to remember Rachel Carson*. The New Yorker. https://www.newyorker.com/magazine/2018/03/26/the-right-way-to-remember-rachel-carson

12   Stoll, M. (2020). *The US federal government responds*. Environment & Society Portal. https://www.environmentandsociety.org/exhibitions/rachel-carsons-silent-spring/us-federal-government-responds

13   Stoll, M. (2020). *The personal attacks on Rachel Carson as a woman scientist*. Environment & Society Portal. https://www.environmentandsociety.org/exhibitions/rachel-carsons-silent-spring/personal-attacks-rachel-carson-woman-scientist

14   *The hero in you* (n.d.). Ellis Paul. https://www.ellispaul.com/songs/The_Hero_In_You/5631/

15   *Silent spring: An environmental revolution* (n.d.). Rachel Carson: Power of the Pen. https://84020520.weebly.com/silent-spring-an-environmental-revolution.html

16   McKie, R. (2010, June 26). *Jane Goodall: 50 years working with chimps | Discover interview*. The Guardian. https://www.theguardian.com/science/2010/jun/27/jane-goodall-chimps-africa-interview

17   Karbo, K. (2018). *In praise of difficult women: Life lessons from 29 heroines who dared to break the rules*. National Geographic Books, p. 177.

18   Based on student responses in the classes Kashwan has taught over the years.

19   Dan, A. (2017, May 11). *Dove invented "Femvertising" but its latest stunt didn't wash with consumers*. Forbes. https://www.forbes.com/sites/avidan/2017/05/11/dove-invented-femvertising-but-its-latest-stunt-didnt-wash-with-consumers/

20   Hussey, M. (2012, September 27). *"Ecohuntress" brings call for environmental advocacy to PHCC's peace week*. Tampa Bay Times.

https://www.tampabay.com/news/humaninterest/ecohuntress-brings-call-for-environmental-advocacy-to-phccs-peace-week/1253712/

21 *Who we are* (2023, July 10). Sea Shepherd Global. https://www.seashepherdglobal.org/who-we-are

22 Dauvergne, P. (2018). *Environmentalism of the rich*. MIT Press, p. 146.

23 *In numbers: Lethal attacks against defenders since 2012* (2023). Global Witness. https://www.globalwitness.org/en/campaigns/environmental-activists/numbers-lethal-attacks-against-defenders-2012/

24 Malkin, E., & Arce, A. (2016, March 4). *Nytimes.com*. The New York Times—Breaking News, US News, World News and Videos. https://www.nytimes.com/2016/03/04/world/americas/berta-caceres-indigenous-activist-is-killed-in-honduras.htmll

25 McVeigh, K. (2022, March 2). *More rights defenders murdered in 2021, with 138 activists killed just in Colombia*. The Guardian. https://www.theguardian.com/global-development/2022/mar/02/more-human-rights-defenders-murdered-2021-environmental-indigenous-rights-activists

26 Battiata, M. (1986, January 25). The Washington Post. https://www.washingtonpost.com/archive/lifestyle/1986/01/25/dian-fossey-the-crusade-the-conflict-the-night-of-horror/7dab897d-3933-4ebf-9a17-263610b1758a/

27 Rodrigues, M. (2019, September 20). *It's time to stop lionizing Dian Fossey as a conservation hero—Lady science*. Lady Science. https://www.ladyscience.com/ideas/time-to-stop-lionizing-dian-fossey-conservation

28 Osterath, B. (2015, December 26). *Gorilla researcher in the mist*. DW. https://www.dw.com/en/dian-fossey-gorilla-researcher-in-the-mist/a-18937282

29 McPherson, A. (2014, January 18). *Zoologist Dian Fossey: A storied life with gorillas*. National Geographic. https://www.nationalgeographic.com/adventure/article/140116-dian-fossey-google-doodle-national-geographic-gorillas-birthday

30 Shoumatoff, A. (1995, January 1). *The fatal obsession of Dian Fossey*. Vanity Fair. https://www.vanityfair.com/style/1986/09/fatal-obsession-198609

31 Kashwan, P. *et al.* (2021). "From racialized neocolonial global conservation to an inclusive and regenerative conservation," *Environment*, 63(4), pp. 4–19.

32 Seasholes, B. (2014, January 16). *Google "Doodle" celebrates cruelty and colonialism*. Reason Foundation. https://reason.org/commentary/google-doodle-celebrates-cruelty-an/

33 Battiata, The Washington Post.

34 *Starbucks stories & news* (2015, April 2). https://stories.starbucks.com/stories/2015/starbucks-ethical-sourcing-program/

35 *Starbucks stories & news* (2018, September 6). https://stories.starbucks.com/press/2018/starbucks-stores-japan-celebrate-99-percent-ethically-sourced-coffee-2018/

36 Starbucks Coffee Company (n.d.). *Ethical sourcing*. https://www.starbucks.com/responsibility/sourcing/coffeee

37 *Starbucks stories & news* (2015, December 1). https://stories.starbucks.com/stories/2015/making-coffee-the-worlds-first-sustainably-sourced-agriculture-product/

38 Badore, M. (2018, October 11). *Starbucks says it now serves "99 percent ethically sourced coffee." So what does that mean?* Treehugger. https://www.treehugger.com/starbucks-says-it-now-serves-percent-ethically-sourced-coffee-so-what-does-mean-4857986

39 Studiolake-dev. (2016, April 8). *Stand challenges Starbucks on four billion cups trashed each year*. Stand.earth. https://www.stand.earth/latest/markets-vs-climate/disposable-cups/stand-challenges-starbucks-four-billion-cups-trashed-each

40 Dewan, A. (2024, February 8). *The world just marked a year above a critical climate limit scientists have warned about*. CNN. https://www.cnn.com/2024/02/08/climate/global-warming-limit-climate-intl/index.htmll

41 McLendon, R. (2023, October 3). *We've been overlooking a major part of climate change, and it's sending warning signs*. ScienceAlert. https://

www.sciencealert.com/weve-been-overlooking-a-major-part-of-climate-change-and-its-sending-warning-signss

42 Yale Environment 360 (2024, March 8). *Great Barrier Reef sees mass bleaching as ocean temperatures hit record high*. Yale E360. https://e360.yale.edu/digest/climate-change-great-barrier-reef-bleaching-20244

43 Richardson, K., Steffen, W., Lucht, W., Bendtsen, J., Cornell, S. E., Donges, J. F., Drüke, M., Fetzer, I., Bala, G., von Bloh, W., & Feulner, G. (2023). "Earth beyond six of nine planetary boundaries," *Science Advances*, 9(37).

44 Tuck, E., & Yang, K. Wayne (2012). "Decolonization is not a metaphor," *Decolonization: Indigeneity, education & society*, 1, pp. 1–40.

45 Bhambra, G. K., & Newell, P. (2022). "More than a metaphor: 'climate colonialism' in perspective," *Global Social Challenges Journal*, 2(2), pp. 1–9.

Chapter 2

1 Mignolo, W., & Walsh, C. (2018). *On decoloniality: concepts, analytics, and praxis*. Duke University Press.

2 Younes, L., Kofman, A., Shaw, A., Song, L., Miller, M., & Flynn, K. (2021, November 2). *Poison in the air*. ProPublica. https://www.propublica.org/article/toxmap-poison-in-the-air

3 Gopal, T. (2023, August 3). *"We are being poisoned": Black residents living in Louisiana's "Cancer alley" say the state is guilty of "genocide" and environmental racism*. Business Insider. https://www.businessinsider.com/cancer-alley-louisiana-epa-environmental-racism-pollution-2023-7

4 Redford, K. (2019, April 5). *The World Bank is no longer above the law*. EarthRights International. https://earthrights.org/blog/the-world-is-watching-how-a-petrochemical-giant-denies-its-neighbors-justicee

5 Sguazzin, A. (2020, March 16). *Bloomberg—Are you a robot?* Bloomberg. https://www.bloomberg.com/news/features/2020-03-17/south-africa-living-near-the-world-s-biggest-emitting-plantt

6   Kershner, I. (2004). *Star wars episode V: The empire strikes back.*
     Beverly Hills, CA, Twentieth Century Fox Home Entertainment.

7   Bullard, R. D. (1993). *Confronting environmental racism: Voices from
     the grassroots.* South End Press, p. 31.

8   Cole, L. W., & Foster, S. R. (2020). *From the ground up: Environmental
     racism and the rise of the environmental justice movement.* New York
     University Press, p. 20.

9   Perkins, T. (2021). "The multiple people of color origins of the US
     environmental justice movement: Social movement spillover and
     regional racial projects in California," *Environmental Sociology,* 7(2),
     pp. 147–59.

10   Estes, N. (2019). *Our history is the future: Standing Rock versus the
     Dakota Access Pipeline, and the long tradition of Indigenous resistance.*
     Verso Books.

11   Gilio-Whitaker, D. (2019). *As long as grass grows: The Indigenous fight
     for environmental justice, from colonization to Standing Rock.* Beacon
     Press.

12   Van Rossum, M. (2022). *The green amendment: The people's fight for a
     clean, safe, and healthy environment.* Disruption Books.

13   Taylor, D. E. (2015). "Gender and racial diversity in environmental
     organizations: Uneven accomplishments and cause for concern,"
     Environmental Justice, 8(5), pp. 165–80.

14   Snyder, S. L. (2023, October 25). *Modernity. Encyclopedia Britannica.*
     https://www.britannica.com/topic/modernity

15   Baban, F. (2017, December 22). *Modernity and its contradictions.*
     Oxford Research Encyclopedia of International Studies.
     https://oxfordre.com/internationalstudies/display/10.1093/
     acrefore/9780190846626.001.0001/acrefore-9780190846626-e-265

16   The Editors (1998, July 20). *Pyramids of Giza.* Encyclopedia Britannica.
     https://www.britannica.com/topic/Pyramids-of-Giza

17   Eisenstadt, S. N. (2003). *Comparative civilizations and multiple
     modernities (2 vols): A collection of essays.* Brill.

18   Stråth, B., & Wagner, P. (2017). *European modernity. A global approach.*
     Bloomsbury Academic.

19   Mignolo, W. (2011). *The darker side of western modernity: Global futures, decolonial options.* Duke University Press.

20   Said, E. W. (1978). *Orientalism.* Pantheon Books, p. 7.

21   Said, *Orientalism,* p. 7.

22   Ghosh, A. (2022). *The nutmeg's curse: Parables for a planet in crisis.* John Murray.

23   *LARB* (2021, November 8). LA Review of Books. https://lareviewofbooks.org/article/the-earth-is-doing-our-thinking-for-us-a-conversation-with-amitav-ghosh//

24   The Editors (2024, March 3). *East India Company.* Encyclopedia Britannica. https://www.britannica.com/topic/East-India-Company

25   Ghosh, *The nutmeg's curse,* p. 118.

26   The Editors, *East India Company.*

27   Robinson, C. (1984). *Black Marxism: The making of the Black radical tradition.* Zed Books; Melamed, J. (2015) "Racial capitalism," *Critical Ethnic Studies,* 1(1), pp. 76–85.

28   Fanon, F. (1961). *The wretched of the earth.* Grove Press.

29   Wa Thiong'o, N. (1986). *Decolonising the mind: The politics of language in African literature.* Currey.

30   Gaventa, J. (1982). *Power and powerlessness: Quiescence and rebellion in an Appalachian valley.* University of Illinois Press.

31   White, J. R. (2022). "Colonizing the American Psyche," in *Critical Theory and Psychoanalysis.* Routledge, pp. 211–30.

32   Bridge, G. (2015, October 27). *The hole world: Scales and spaces of extraction.* Scenario Journal. https://scenariojournal.com/article/the-hole-world/

33   Hartwick, B., & Brechin, G. (2001). "Imperial San Francisco: Urban power, earthly ruin," *Economic Geography,* 77(4), p. 388.

34   Bridge, *The hole world.*

35   Chagnon, C. W., Durante, F., Gills, B. K., Hagolani-Albov, S. E., Hokkanen, S., Kangasluoma, S. M., Konttinen, H., Kröger, M., LaFleur, W., Ollinaho, O., & Vuola, M. P. (2022). "From extractivism to global extractivism: The evolution of an organizing concept," *The Journal of*

Peasant Studies, 49(4), pp. 760–92. https://doi.org/10.1080/03066150.2 022.2069015

36 See these examples: Deletter, E. (2023, August 16). *Apple agrees to pay up to $500 million in settlement over slowed-down iPhones: What to know*. USA Today. https://www.usatoday.com/story/money/2023/08/16/ apple-500-million-dollar-iphone-settlement/70600993007; Leyvraz, S. (2023, December 27). *Right to repair and the fight against planned obsolescence*. Bot Populi. https://botpopuli.net/right-to-repair-and-the-fight-against-planned-obsolescence/

37 Green, A. (2021, May 13). *You're not crazy: Your appliances were built to fail you*. PIRG. https://pirg.org/articles/youre-not-crazy-your-appliances-were-built-to-fail-you/

38 Dussel, E. (1993). "Eurocentrism and modernity (introduction to the Frankfurt lectures)," *Boundary*, 20(3), p. 65.

39 Wagner, P. (2012). *Progress: A reconstruction*. Polity Press.

40 Sankey, K., & Munck, R. (2016). "Rethinking development in Latin America: The search for alternative paths in the twenty-first century," *Journal of Developing Societies*, 32(4), pp. 334–61.

41 Rincón, L. F., & Fernandes, B. M. (2018). "Territorial dispossession: Dynamics of capitalist expansion in rural territories in South America," *Third World Quarterly*, 39(11), pp. 2085–102; Watts, M. (2017). "Resource curse? Governmentality, oil and power in the Niger delta, Nigeria," in *Environment*. Routledge, pp. 503–33.

42 *Standing Rock Sioux and Dakota access pipeline | Teacher resource* (n.d.). National Museum of the American Indian. https://americanindian. si.edu/nk360/plains-treaties/dapll

43 Flores, R. K., Böhm, S., & Misoczky, M. C. (2022). "Contesting extractivism: International business and people's struggles against extractive industries," *Critical Perspectives on International Business*, 18(1), pp. 1–14.

44 Calma, J. (2023, June 6). *Why violence against women environmental defenders is undercounted*. The Verge. https://www.theverge. com/2023/6/6/23751071/violence-against-women-environmental-activists-data-researchh

45 Atiles, J., & Rojas-Páez, G. (2022). "Coal criminals: Crimes of the powerful, extractivism and historical harm in the global south," *The British Journal of Criminology*, 62(5), pp. 1289–304; Penados, F., Gahman, L., & Smith, S.-J. (2022). "Land, race, and (slow) violence: Indigenous resistance to racial capitalism and the coloniality of development in the Caribbean," *Geoforum; Journal of Physical, Human, and Regional Geosciences*, 145.

46 Lakhani, N., Gayle, D., & Taylor, M. (2023, October 12). *How criminalisation is being used to silence climate activists across the world.* The Guardian. https://www.theguardian.com/environment/2023/oct/12/how-criminalisation-is-being-used-to-silence-climate-activists-across-the-world

47 Dunlap, A. (2023). "The structures of conquest: Debating extractivism(s), infrastructures and environmental justice for advancing post-development pathways," *International Development Policy*, 16(16).

48 Wa Thiong'o, *Decolonising the mind*, p. 2.

49 Wiedmann, T., Lenzen, M., Keyßer, L. T., & Steinberger, J. K. (2020). "Scientists' warning on affluence," *Nature Communications*, 11(1), p. 3107.

50 Gupta, J., Liverman, D., Prodani, K., Aldunce, P., Bai, X., Broadgate, W., Ciobanu, D., Gifford, L., Gordon, C., Hurlbert, M., Inoue, C. Y. A., Jacobson, L., Kanie, N., Lade, S. J., Lenton, T. M., Obura, D., Okereke, C., Otto, I. M., Pereira, L., Rockström, J., Scholtens, J., Rocha, J., Stewart-Koster, B., Tàbara, J. D., Rammelt C., & Verburg, P.H. (2023). "Earth system justice needed to identify and live within Earth system boundaries," *Nature Sustainability*, 6, p. 1–9.

51 Kashwan, P. (2020, September 2). *American environmentalism's racist roots have shaped global thinking about conservation.* The Conversation. https://theconversation.com/american-environmentalisms-racist-roots-have-shaped-global-thinking-about-conservation-143783

52 Hankins, D. L. (2015). "Restoring Indigenous prescribed fires to California oak woodlands," in *Proceedings of the seventh California oak symposium: Managing oak woodlands in a dynamic world. Gen.*

Tech. Rep. PSW-GTR-251. Department of Agriculture, Forest Service, Pacific Southwest Research Station, p. 579.

53 Avitt, A. (2021, November 16). *Tribal and Indigenous fire tradition.* US Forest Service. https://www.fs.usda.gov/features/tribal-and-indigenous-fire-traditionn

54 Fanon, F. (1970). *A dying colonialism.* Penguin.

55 Lloyd, G. (1984). *Man of reason: Male and female in western philosophy.* Routledge.

56 Bhambra, G. K., & Newell, P. (2022). "More than a metaphor: 'Climate colonialism' in perspective," *Global Social Challenges Journal*, 2(2), pp. 1–9.

57 Green, F., & Healy, N. (2022). "How inequality fuels climate change: The climate case for a Green New Deal," *One Earth*, 5(6), pp. 635–49.

58 Gilio-Whitaker, *As long as grass grows: The Indigenous fight for environmental justice, from colonization to Standing Rock*; Schneider, L. (2022). "'Land back' beyond repatriation: Restoring Indigenous land relationships," in *The Routledge companion to gender and the American west.* Routledge, pp. 452–64.

59 Van Rossum, *The green amendment: The people's fight for a clean, safe, and healthy environment.*

60 Giddens, A. (1998). *Conversations with Anthony Giddens: Making Sense of Modernity.* Stanford University Press.

Chapter 3

1 Stephens, J. C. *et al.* (2021). "The risks of solar geoengineering research," *Science (New York, N.Y.)*, 372(6547), p. 1161.

2 Rowell, A., & Evans-Reeves, K. (2017, April 7). *It was Big Tobacco, not Trump, that wrote the post-truth rule book.* The Conversation. https://theconversation.com/it-was-big-tobacco-not-trump-that-wrote-the-post-truth-rule-book-75782; Brownell, K. D., & Warner, K. E. (2009). "The perils of ignoring history: Big Tobacco played dirty and millions died. How similar is Big Food?," *The Milbank quarterly*, 87(1), pp. 259–94.

3   Kanakia, R. (2007, February 13). *Tobacco companies obstructed science, history professor says.* Stanford News. https://news.stanford.edu/pr/2007/pr-proctor-021407.html

4   Black, S., Liu, A., Parry, I., & Vernon, N. (2023, August 24). *IMF fossil fuel subsidies data: 2023 update.* IMF. https://www.imf.org/en/Publications/WP/Issues/2023/08/22/IMF-Fossil-Fuel-Subsidies-Data-2023-Update-537281

5   Dunlap, R. E., & McCright, A. M. (2011). *Organized climate change denial.* Oxford University Press.

6   Fugleberg, J. (2013, June 10). *Emails: University of Wyoming officials sped up, touted removal of anti-coal sculpture.* Casper Star-Tribune. https://trib.com/business/energy/emails-university-of-wyoming-officials-sped-up-touted-removal-of/article_4f9332ee-d83c-5d58-a38b-19e913ba739d.html

7   Lamb, W. F. *et al.* (2020). "Discourses of climate delay," *Global sustainability*, 3(e17).

8   McMahon, J. (2017, September 24). *As humans fumble climate challenge, interest grows in geoengineering.* Forbes. https://www.forbes.com/sites/jeffmcmahon/2017/09/24/interest-rises-in-geoengineering-as-humans-fail-to-mitigate-climate-change/?sh=220a96576472

9   Haywood, C. (2018, November 14). *Burning to solve climate change: The BECCS paradox.* Business Green | News and Analysis for the Low Carbon Economy. https://www.businessgreen.com/bg/opinion/3065711/burning-to-solve-climate-change-the-beccs-paradox

10   Irvine, P. J., Sriver, R. L., & Keller, K. (2012). "Tension between reducing sea-level rise and global warming through solar-radiation management," *Nature Climate Change*, 2(2), pp. 97–100; Tilmes, S. *et al.* (2013). "The hydrological impact of geoengineering in the Geoengineering Model Intercomparison Project (GeoMIP): THE HYDROLOGIC IMPACT OF GEOENGINEERING," *Journal of Geophysical Research Atmospheres*, 118(19), pp. 11,036–58.

11   *Pollution weakens monsoon's might: Local, global emissions suppress South Asian summer rainfall* (2012, July 13). Earth & Environmental Systems Modeling | Earth & Environmental Systems Modeling. https://climatemodeling.science.energy.gov/research-highlights/

pollution-weakens-monsoons-might-local-global-emissions-suppress-south-asian; Kashwan, P. (2018, December 29). *India should demand global, political oversight for geoengineering R&D*. Business Standard. https://www.business-standard.com/article/current-affairs/india-should-demand-global-political-oversight-for-geoengineering-r-d-118122900154_1.htmll

12 Levitt, T. (2017, September 20). *Demand for biofuels is increasing global food prices, says study*. The Guardian. https://www.theguardian.com/sustainable-business/2017/sep/20/demand-for-biofuels-is-increasing-global-food-prices-says-studyy

13 Frase, P. (2017, August 15). *By any means necessary*. Jacobin. https://jacobinmag.com/2017/08/by-any-means-necessary/

14 Robock, A., Jerch, K., & Bunzl, M. (2008) "20 reasons why geoengineering may be a bad idea," *The Bulletin of the Atomic Scientists*, 64(2), pp. 14–59.

15 Chhetri, N., Chong, D., Conca, K., Falk, R., Gillespie, A., Gupta, A., Jinnah, S., Kashwan, P., Lahsen, M., & Light, A. (2018). "Governing solar radiation management, forum for climate engineering assessment," American University, Washington; Stephens, J. C., Kashwan, P., McLaren, D., & Surprise, K. (2021). "The dangers of mainstreaming solar geoengineering: A critique of the national academies report," *Environmental Politics*, 32(1), p. 1–10.

16 Wainwright, J., & Mann, G. (2020). *Climate leviathan: A political theory of our planetary future*. Verso Books.

17 Biermann, F. *et al.* (2022). "Solar geoengineering: The case for an international non-use agreement," *Wiley Interdisciplinary Reviews. Climate Change*, 13(3).

18 Stephens, J. C., & Surprise, K. (2020). "The hidden injustices of advancing solar geoengineering research," *Global sustainability*, 3(e2).

19 McCright, A. M., & Dunlap, R. E. (2011). "Cool dudes: The denial of climate change among conservative white males in the United States," *Global Environmental Change: Human and Policy Dimensions*, 21(4), pp. 1163–72.

20 Lewis, Simon L., & Maslin, Mark A. (2015). "Defining the Anthropocene," *Nature*, 519(7542), pp. 171–80.

21 *Anthropocene* (n.d.). National Geographic Society. https://www. nationalgeographic.org/encyclopedia/anthropocene/

22 Samuel, S. (2024, March 20). *Why did geologists reject the "Anthropocene" epoch? It's not rock science.* Vox. https://www.vox.com/ future-perfect/2024/3/7/24092675/anthropocene-climate-change- epoch-geology

23 Witnessed by Prakash Kashwan, who also spoke at the workshop.

24 Yoon, S., & Amadiegwu, A. (2023, June 22). *What are some of the innovations that could become game changers for net zero?* World Economic Forum. https://www.weforum.org/agenda/2023/06/these- new-technologies-will-accelerate-the-transition-to-net-zero/

25 Haraway, D. *et al.* (2016). "Anthropologists are talking—about the anthropocene," *Ethnos*, 81(3), pp. 535–64.

26 Davis, J., Moulton, A. A., Van Sant, L., & Williams, B. (2019). "Anthropocene, capitalocene, … plantationocene?: A manifesto for ecological justice in an age of global crises," *Geography Compass*, 13(5).

27 Capitalocene is favored by several scholars namely Malm, Andreas, Moore, Jason, & Haraway, Donna. For details see: Moore, Jason W. (2016). *Anthropocene or Capitalocene?: Nature, history, and the crisis of capitalism.* PM Press; Haraway, D. (2015). "Anthropocene, Capitalocene, Plantationocene, Chthulucene: Making kin," *Environmental Humanities*, 6(1), pp. 159–65.

28 Revkin, A. C. (2008, May 2). *Poetry and air, imagery and earth.* Dot Earth Blog. https://archive.nytimes.com/dotearth.blogs.nytimes. com/2008/05/02/poetry-and-air-imagery-and-earth/

29 Bauman, Z. (2014). *Wasted lives: Modernity and its outcasts.* Polity Press.

30 Editorial Board (2022, August 31). *Chile should send its proposed constitution back for a rewrite.* The Washington Post. https://www. washingtonpost.com/opinions/2022/08/31/chile-constitution-vote- reject-rewrite/

31 Dunlap, A. (2018, May 10). *End the "Green" delusions: Industrial- scale renewable energy is fossil.* Verso. https://www.versobooks.com/

blogs/3797-end-the-green-delusions-industrial-scale-renewable-
energy-is-fossil-fuell

32   Harvey, David (2007). "Neoliberalism as creative destruction," *The Annals of the American Academy of Political and Social Science*, 610(1), pp. 21–44.

33   *Record number of fossil fuel lobbyists at COP undermines critical climate talks* (2023, December 5). Amnesty International. https://www. amnesty.org/en/latest/news/2023/12/global-record-number-of-fossil-fuel-lobbyists-at-cop-undermines-critical-climate-talks/

34   Wainwright & Mann, *Climate leviathan*.

35   Wainwright & Mann, *Climate leviathan*.

36   Bashford, A., & Chaplin, J. E. (2016). *The New Worlds of Thomas Robert Malthus: Rereading the "Principle of Population."* Princeton University Press.

37   Crist, E., Ripple, W. J., Ehrlich, P. R., Rees, W. E., & Wolf, C. (2022). "Scientists' warning on population," *Science of the Total Environment*, 845, p. 157166.

38   Wiedmann, T., Lenzen, M., Keyßer, L. T., & Steinberger, J. K. (2020). "Scientists' warning on affluence," *Nature Communications*, 11(1), p. 3107.

Chapter 4

1   Brundtland, G. H., & World Commission on Environment and Development (1990). *Our common future: The commission for the future, world commission on environment and development.* OUP Australia.

2   Carlowitz, Hans Carl von (2022[1713]). *Sylvicultura Oeconomica.* Legare Street Press.

3   Du Pisani, Jacobus A., Professor (2006). "Sustainable development—historical roots of the concept," *Environmental Sciences*, 3(2), pp. 83–96.

4   USFS (n.d.). *The greatest good: A forest service Centennial film.* https://www.fs.usda.gov/greatestgood/press/mediakit/facts/history.

shtml?sub3#:~:text=Dietrich%20Brandis%2C%20a%20world-renowned,of%20a%20federal%20forestry%20organization

5   These arrangements are known as either Burmese Agroforestry, or simply Begar, which is a Hindi word for unpaid labor.

6   Gururani, S. (2002). "Forests of pleasure and pain: Gendered practices of labor and livelihood in the forests of the Kumaon Himalayas, India," *Gender, Place and Culture: A Journal of Feminist Geography*, 9(3), pp. 229–43.

7   Kashwan, P. (2017). *Democracy in the woods: Environmental conservation and social justice in India, Tanzania, and Mexico*. Oxford University Press.

8   Etchart, L. (2017). "The role of Indigenous Peoples in combating climate change," *Palgrave Communications*, 3(1), p. 17085.

9   Verrier, E. (1958). *Leaves from the Jungle: Life in a Gond Village*. 2nd ed. London, England: Oxford University Press.

10   Kashwan, P. (2017). "Inequality, democracy, and the environment: A cross-national analysis," *Ecological Economics: The Journal of the International Society for Ecological Economics*, 131, pp. 139–51.

11   Schultz, B. *et al.* (2022). "Recognizing the equity implications of restoration priority maps," *Environmental Research Letters*, 17(11).

12   Fleischman, F. D. (2012). *Public servant behavior and forest policy implementation in Central India*. Indiana University Press.

13   Kashwan, P. (2013). "The politics of rights-based approaches in conservation," *Land Use Policy*, 31, pp. 613–26.

14   Kashwan, P. (2017, November 15). *Bigotry against Indigenous People means we're missing a trick on climate change*. The Guardian. https://www.theguardian.com/working-in-development/2017/nov/15/bigotry-against-indigenous-people-means-were-missing-a-trick-on-climate-change

15   Sène, A. L. (2023). "Justice in nature conservation: Limits and possibilities under global capitalism," *Climate and Development*, pp. 1–10.

16   Colchester, M. (2016). "Do commodity certification systems uphold Indigenous Peoples' rights? Lessons from the Roundtable on Sustainable Palm Oil and Forest Stewardship Council," *Policy Matters*, 21, pp. 150–65.

17 Tollefson, J., & Gilbert, N. (2012). "Earth summit: Rio report card," *Nature*, 486(7401), pp. 20–3.

18 UN (n.d.). *The 17 goals*. Sustainable Development. https://sdgs.un.org/goals

19 Pedersen, C. S. (2018). "The UN sustainable development goals (SDGs) are a great gift to business!," *Procedia CIRP*, 69, pp. 21–4.

20 Nogrady, B. (2020, June 17). *Cobalt is critical to the renewable energy transition. How can we minimize its social and environmental cost?* New Security Beat. https://www.newsecuritybeat.org/2020/06/cobalt-critical-renewable-energy-transition-minimize-social-environmental-cost

21 Lakhani, N. (2023, January 24). *Revealed: How US transition to electric cars threatens environmental havoc.* The Guardian. https://www.theguardian.com/us-news/2023/jan/24/us-electric-vehicles-lithium-consequences-research

22 Mossalgue, J. (2024, February 6). *Turns out, Europeans love big ol' SUVs as much as Americans do.* Electrek. https://electrek.co/2024/02/06/turns-out-europeans-love-big-ol-suvs-as-much-as-americans-do/

23 *EVs keep getting bigger—and that could steer the U.S. down a dangerous road* (2022, July 10). FastCompany.com. https://www.fastcompany.com/90793619/evs-keep-getting-bigger-and-that-could-steer-the-u-s-down-a-dangerous-road

24 Katwala, A. (2018). *The spiralling environmental cost of our lithium battery addiction.* WIRED UK. https://www.wired.co.uk/article/lithium-batteries-environment-impact.

25 Kumar, M. (2015, September 10). *Human development: Meaning, objectives and components.* Economics Discussion. https://www.economicsdiscussion.net/human-development/human-development-meaning-objectives-and-components/11754

26 Henry, LaVaughn M. (2014). "Income inequality and income-class consumption patterns," *Federal Reserve Bank of Cleveland, Economic Commentary 2014–18*. https://doi.org/10.26509/frbc-ec-201418.

27 We use scare quotes to point out that it is no longer politically correct to use this phrase that divides our beloved humanity into

three hierarchical groups, a classification that is demeaning for those relegated to the "third" world.

28 The American Human Development index is published by an independent project, The Measure of America, which has been supported by the Social Science Research Council (SSRC) since 2008. Measure of America (MoA) (2019, March 29). *About the project*. Measure of America: A Program of the Social Science Research Council. https://measureofamerica.org/project/

29 *Adult literacy in the United States* (2019, July). National Center for Education Statistics (NCES), a part of the U.S. Department of Education. https://nces.ed.gov/pubs2019/2019179/index.asp

30 Davies, D. (2020, November 23). *"Waste" activist digs into the sanitation crisis affecting the rural poor*. NPR. https://www.npr.org/sections/health-shots/2020/11/23/937945160/waste-activist-digs-into-the-sanitation-crisis-affecting-the-rural-poor'

31 Greenwood, D. T., & Holt, R. P. F. (2010). "Growth, inequality and negative trickle down," *Journal of Economic Issues*, 44(2), pp. 403–10.

32 Kallis, G. (2011). "In defence of degrowth," *Ecological Economics: The Journal of the International Society for Ecological Economics*, 70(5), pp. 873–80.

33 Sutoris, P. (2021, November 7). *Infinite economic growth caused the environmental crisis. Degrowth will help us fix it*. Salon. https://www.salon.com/2021/11/07/infinite-economic-growth-caused-the-environmental-crisis-degrowth-will-help-us-fix-it

34 Watson, S. K. (2021, July 6). *What is "degrowth" and how can it fight climate change?* Popular Science. https://www.popsci.com/environment/what-is-degrowth-and-how-can-it-fight-climate-change

35 Demaria, F. *et al.* (2013). "What is degrowth? From an activist slogan to a social movement," *Environmental Values*, 22(2), pp. 191–215.

36 Schmelzer, M., Vetter, A., & Vansintjan, A. (2022). *The future is degrowth: A guide to a world beyond capitalism*. Edited by M. Schmelzer, A. Vetter, & A. Vansintjan.Verso Books.

37 Mehta, L., & Harcourt, W. (2021). "Beyond limits and scarcity: Feminist and decolonial contributions to degrowth," *Political Geography*, 89(102411), p. 102411.

38 Hickel, J. (2021). "The anti-colonial politics of degrowth," *Political geography*, 88(102404).

39 Jaffee, D. (2014, xv). *Brewing justice: Fair trade coffee, sustainability, and survival*. University of California Press.

40 Taylor, P. L. (2005). "In the market but not of it: Fair trade coffee and forest stewardship council certification as market-based social change," *World Development*, 33(1), pp. 129–47.

41 Renard, M.-C. (2005). "Quality certification, regulation and power in fair trade," *Journal of Rural Studies*, 21(4), pp. 419–31.

42 Beuchelt, T. D., & Zeller, M. (2011). "Profits and poverty: Certification's troubled link for Nicaragua's organic and fairtrade coffee producers," *Ecological Economics: The Journal of the International Society for Ecological Economics*, 70(7), pp. 1316–24.

43 Besky, S. (2014). *The Darjeeling distinction: Labor and justice on fair-trade tea plantations in India* (Vol. 47). University of California Press.

44 Sylla, N. (2014). *The fair trade scandal: Marketing poverty to benefit the rich*. Ohio University Press.

45 Zizek, S. (2018). *First as tragedy, then as farce*. Verso Books.

46 Ward, B. (2020, March 3). "Rina Sawayama Pokes Fun at Capitalist Ignorance on '00s-Inspired Pop Cut 'XS.'" *DMY*. https://dmy.co/new-music/rina-sawayama-xs.

47 Stafford, R. (2019). "Sustainability: A flawed concept for fisheries management?," *Elementa (Washington, D.C.)*, 7(1), p. 8.; Boluk, K. A., Cavaliere, C. T., & Higgins-Desbiolles, F. (2021). "A critical framework for interrogating the United Nations Sustainable Development Goals 2030 Agenda in tourism," in *Activating critical thinking to advance the sustainable development goals in tourism systems*. Routledge, pp. 1–18.

48 Anantharaman, M. (2024). *Recycling class: The contradictions of inclusion in urban sustainability*. MIT Press.

49   Agyeman, J., Bullard, R. D., & Evans, B. (2002). "Exploring the nexus: Bringing together sustainability, environmental justice and equity," *Space and Polity*, 6(1), pp. 77–90.

50   Sze, J. (ed.) (2020). *Sustainability: Approaches to environmental justice and social power*. New York University Press.

51   Agyeman, Bullard, & Evans, "Exploring the nexus," pp. 77–90, p. 3.

52   Harvey, D. (1982). *The limits to capital*. Blackwell.

Chapter 5

1   Pearce, F. (2011, June 1). *Dark earth: How humans enriched the rainforests*. New Scientist. https://www.newscientist.com/article/mg21028151-800-dark-earth-how-humans-enriched-the-rainforests/

2   Science News (2016, June 16). *700-year-old west African soil technique could help mitigate climate change*. ScienceDaily. https://www.sciencedaily.com/releases/2016/06/160616105901.htm

3   The Royal Society (2021, February 2). *David Attenborough and Venki Ramakrishnan on the Dasgupta Review*. YouTube. https://www.youtube.com/watch?v=e2QDOeKH0DE

4   Kashwan, P., Kukreti, I., & Ranjan, R. (2021). "The UN declaration on the rights of peasants, national policies, and forestland rights of India's Adivasis," *The International Journal of Human Rights*, 25(7), pp. 1184–209.

5   Rainforest Foundation UK (2016, January 1). *Reserved! An atlas on Indigenous Peoples facing nature conservation*. Academia.edu—Share research. https://www.academia.edu/41503220/Reserved_An_Atlas_on_Indigenous_Peoples_facing_Nature_Conservation

6   Kennedy, C. M. *et al.* (2023). "Indigenous Peoples' lands are threatened by industrial development; conversion risk assessment reveals need to support Indigenous stewardship," *One earth (Cambridge, Mass.)*, 6(8), pp. 1032–49.

7   Tauli-Corpuz, V., Alcorn, J., & Molnar, A. (n.d.). *Brief*. Cornered by PAs. https://www.corneredbypas.com/brief

8   Purdy, J. (2015, August 13). *Environmentalism's racist history*.
     The New Yorker. https://www.newyorker.com/news/news-desk/
     environmentalisms-racist-history

9   De Bont, R. (2015). "'Primitives' and protected areas: International
     conservation and the 'naturalization' of Indigenous People, ca. 1910–
     1975," *Journal of the History of Ideas*, 76(2), pp. 215–36, p. 218.

10   Neumann, R. P. (2000). "Land, justice, and the politics of conservation
     in Tanzania," in *People, plants, and justice: The politics of nature
     conservation*. Columbia University Press.

11   Dowie, M. (2011). *Conservation refugees: The hundred-year conflict
     between global conservation and native peoples*. MIT Press.

12   Tidnam, H. E. (2016, August 26). *National parks are beautiful—but the
     way they were created isn't*. Medium. https://timeline.com/national-
     parks-native-americans-56b0dad62c9d

13   Raymond, H. (2007). "The ecologically noble savage debate," *Annual
     Review of Anthropology*, 36(1), pp. 177–90.

14   Raymond, "The ecologically noble savage debate," pp. 177–90, p. 177.

15   Raymond, "The ecologically noble savage debate," pp. 177–90, pp.
     181–2.

16   Raymond, "The ecologically noble savage debate," pp. 177–90, p. 185.

17   Raymond, "The ecologically noble savage debate," pp. 177–90.

18   Fischer, A., & Young, J. C. (2007). "Understanding mental constructs
     of biodiversity: Implications for biodiversity management and
     conservation," *Biological Conservation*, 136(2), pp. 271–82.

19   Sandbrook, C. *et al.* (2010). "Carbon, forests and the REDD paradox,"
     Oryx: The Journal of the Fauna Preservation Society, 44(3), pp.
     330–34.

20   Cascais, A. (2019, May 16). *Our ancestors entrusted this forest to us*.
     DW. https://www.dw.com/en/nature-conservation-projects-marred-by-
     human-rights-violations/a-48765516

21   Cited in Chapin, M. (2004). "A challenge to conservationists," *World
     Watch Magazine* (November/December 2004), pp. 17–31.

22   Cited in Chapin, "A challenge to conservationists," pp. 17–31, p. 17.

23   Cited in Chapin, "A challenge to conservationists," pp. 17–31, p. 29.

24 Dowie, M. (2009, November 25). *Conservation: Indigenous People's enemy No. 1?* Mother Jones. https://www.motherjones.com/environment/2009/11/conservation-indigenous-peoples-enemy-no-1/

25 About Us (n.d.). *Conservation initiative on human rights.* CIHR. https://www.thecihr.org/

26 Campese, J. (2009). *Rights-based approaches: Exploring issues and opportunities for conservation.* Center for International Forestry Research.

27 Greiber, T. *et al.* (2010). "Conservation with justice: A rights-based approach" (Italics added for emphasis).

28 Tauli-Corpuz, V. *et al.* (2020). "Cornered by PAs: Adopting rights-based approaches to enable cost-effective conservation and climate action," *World development*, 130(104923), p. 104923.

29 UNEP (2017, April 26). *Indigenous People and nature: A tradition of conservation.* https://www.unenvironment.org/news-and-stories/story/indigenous-people-and-nature-tradition-conservation

30 UNEP, *Indigenous People and nature: A tradition of conservation* (Italics added for emphasis).

31 Eghenter, C. (2019, August 9). *Learning conservation from Indigenous People.* WWF conserves our planet, habitats, & species like the Panda & Tiger | WWF. https://wwf.panda.org/knowledge_hub/where_we_work/borneo_forests/?351390/Learning-Conservation-from-Indigenous-People

32 Eghenter, *Learning conservation from Indigenous People.*

33 Kashwan, P. (2013). "The politics of rights-based approaches in conservation," *Land Use Policy*, 31, pp. 613–26.

34 Kashwan, "The Politics of Rights-Based Approaches in Conservation," pp. 613–26, p. 623.

35 Vidal, J. (2016, March 3). *WWF accused of facilitating human rights abuses of tribal people in Cameroon.* The Guardian. https://www.theguardian.com/environment/2016/mar/03/wwf-accused-of-facilitating-human-rights-abuses-of-tribal-people-in-cameroon

36 Rowlatt, J. (2017, February 10). *Kaziranga: The park that shoots people to protect rhinos.* BBC News. https://www.bbc.com/news/world-south-asia-38909512

37   Warren, T., & Baker, K. J. (2019, March 4). *WWF funds guards who have tortured and killed people.* BuzzFeed News. https://www. buzzfeednews.com/article/tomwarren/wwf-world-wide-fund-nature-parks-torture-deathh

38   Engert, M., Baker, K. J., & Warren, T. (2019, July 23). *Germany has stopped funding wildlife charity WWF amid ongoing human rights investigations.* BuzzFeed News. https://www.buzzfeednews.com/article/marcusengert/germany-has-stopped-funding-wildlife-charity-wwf-amid

39   Survival International (2020, October 2). *Atrocities prompt US authorities to halt funding to WWF, WCS in major blow to conservation industry.* https://www.survivalinternational.org/news/12475.

40   Lunstrum, E. (2014). "Green militarization: Anti-poaching efforts and the spatial contours of Kruger National Park," *Annals of the Association of American Geographers*, 104(4), pp. 816–32.

41   Duffy, R., Massé, F., Smidt, E., Marijnen, E., Büscher, B., Verweijen, J., Ramutsindela, M., Simlai, T., Joanny, L., & Lunstrum, E. (2019). "Why we must question the militarisation of conservation," *Biological Conservation*, 232, pp. 66–73.

42   Duffy, R., Dickinson, H., & Joanny, L. (2017, July 12). *Foreign "conservation armies" in Africa may be doing more harm than good.* The Conversation. https://theconversation.com/foreign-conservation-armies-in-africa-may-be-doing-more-harm-than-good-80719

43   Haenlein, C., & Smith, M. L. R. (eds.) (2017). *Poaching, wildlife trafficking and security in Africa: Myths and realities.* Taylor & Francis.

44   Duffy, R. (2014). "Waging a war to save biodiversity: The rise of militarized conservation," *International Affairs*, 90(4), pp. 819–34.

45   Pennaz, A. K., Ahmadou, M., Moritz, M., & Scholte, P. (2018). "Not seeing the cattle for the elephants: The implications of discursive linkages between Boko Haram and wildlife poaching in Waza National Park, Cameroon," *Conservation and Society*, 16(2), pp. 125–35.

46   Felbab-Brown, V. (2018). "Wildlife and drug trafficking, terrorism, and human security," *Prism*, 7(4), pp. 124–37.

47   Marijnen, E., & Verweijen, J. (2016). "Selling green militarization: The discursive (re) production of militarized conservation in the Virunga National Park, Democratic Republic of the Congo," *Geoforum*, 75, pp. 274–85.

48   Hsu, J. (2017, April 5). *The hard truth about the rhino horn "Aphrodisiac" market*. Scientific American. https://www. scientificamerican.com/article/the-hard-truth-about-the-rhino-horn-aphrodisiac-market/

49   Kashwan, P. (2019). *The white hunter. Africa is a country*. https:// africasacountry.com/2019/09/the-white-hunter

50   Brockington, D., & Duffy, R. (eds.) (2011). *Capitalism and conservation*. John Wiley & Sons.

51   Iordăchescu, G., Lappe-Osthege, T., Dickinson, H., Duffy, R., & Burns, C. (2023). "Political ecologies of green-collar crime: Understanding illegal trades in European wildlife," *Environmental Politics*, 32(5), pp. 923–30.

52   Robinson, J. G. (2012). "Common and conflicting interests in the engagements between conservation organizations and corporations," *Conservation Biology*, 26(6), pp. 967–77.

53   Adams, W. M. (2017). "Sleeping with the enemy? Biodiversity conservation, corporations and the green economy," *Journal of Political Ecology*, 24(1), pp. 243–57. https://doi.org/10.2458/v24i1.20804. Visser, I. N., Barefoot, N. N., Law, C., & Spiegl, M. V. (2021). "Wildlife conservation and public relations: the greenwashing of marine mammal captivity," *Editora Artemis*. https://editoraartemis.com. br/catalogo/post/wildlife-conservation-and-public-relations-the-greenwashing-of-marine-mammal-captivity.

54   Nadasdy, P. (2005). "Transcending the debate over the ecologically noble Indian: Indigenous peoples and environmentalism," *Ethnohistory (Columbus, Ohio)*, 52(2), pp. 291–331.

55   Nadasdy, "Transcending the debate over the ecologically noble Indian," pp. 291–331, p. 300.

56   Cabrera, Y. (2021, April 6). *With wildfires on the rise, Indigenous fire management is poised to make a comeback*. Grist. https://grist.org/

justice/with-wildfires-on-the-rise-indigenous-fire-management-is-poised-to-make-a-comeback

57 Kormann, C. (2018, October 10). *How carbon trading became a way of life for California's Yurok Tribe*. The New Yorker. https://www.newyorker.com/news/dispatch/how-carbon-trading-became-a-way-of-life-for-californias-yurok-tribe

58 Kormann, *How carbon trading became a way of life for California's Yurok Tribe*.

59 ICT Staff (2018, September 12). *"Sovereignty by the Barrel": Tribe takes control of oil production*. ICT NEWS. https://indiancountrytoday.com/archive/sovereignty-by-the-barrel-tribe-takes-control-of-oil-production-4F796kUAo0S2GrEx3TfGbw

60 Brandt, K. (2020, June 22). *Sovereignty by the barrel?* Native Science Report. https://nativesciencereport.org/2019/04/sovereignty-by-the-barrel/

61 Golden, H. (2021, February 20). *"Piecing together a broken heart": Native Americans rebuild territories they lost*. The Guardian. https://www.theguardian.com/environment/2021/feb/20/native-americans-rebuild-lost-territories-real-estate

62 Coumans, C. (2010). "Alternative accountability mechanisms and mining: The problems of effective impunity, human rights, and agency," *Revue canadienne d'etudes du developpement [Canadian journal of development studies]*, 30(1–2), pp. 27–48.

63 Kashwan, P. (2015). "Forest policy, institutions, and REDD+ in India, Tanzania, and Mexico," *Global Environmental Politics*, 15(3), pp. 95–117.

64 Fleischman, F. *et al.* (2021). "How politics shapes the outcomes of forest carbon finance," *Current Opinion in Environmental Sustainability*, 51, pp. 7–14.

65 Kashwan, Kukreti, & Ranjan, "The UN declaration on the rights of peasants, national policies, and forestland rights of India's Adivasis," pp. 1184–209.

66 Paschen, T. (2024, January 23). *The conservation sector must communicate better (commentary)*. Mongabay Environmental News. https://news.mongabay.com/2024/01/the-conservation-sector-must-communicate-better-commentary/

67 Reed, J. *et al.* (2020). "The extent and distribution of joint conservation-development funding in the tropics," *One earth (Cambridge, Mass.)*, 3(6), pp. 753–62.

68 Muiruri, P. (2024, January 31). *"We said, there must be ladies": The pioneering Maasai women ending all-male leadership of the land*. The Guardian. https://www.theguardian.com/environment/2024/jan/31/maasai-women-kenyan-wildlife-reserve

69 Blok, A. (2021). "Review of Sustainable materialism: Environmental movements and the politics of everyday life, by David Schlosberg and Luke Craven," *Environmental Politics*, 30(5), pp. 863–5. https://doi.org/10.1080/09644016.2021.1919344

70 Kashwan, Kukreti, & Ranjan, "The UN declaration on the rights of peasants, national policies, and forestland rights of India's Adivasis," pp. 1184–209.

71 Sène, A. L. (2023). "Justice in nature conservation: Limits and possibilities under global capitalism," *Climate and Development*, pp. 1–10.

72 Ferdinand, M. (2022). "Behind the colonial silence of wilderness: 'In marronage lies the search of a world'," *Environmental Humanities*, 14(1), pp. 182–201.

73 Carlisle, L. (2022). *Healing grounds: Climate, justice, and the deep roots of regenerative farming*. Island Press.

74 Sène, A. L. (2024). "A reflection on imperialism in nature conservation from African conceptions of care," *Environmental Communication*, 18(1–2), pp. 15–20.

75 Turnhout, E., Metze, T., Wyborn, C., Klenk, N., & Louder, E. (2020). "The politics of co-production: Participation, power, and transformation," *Current Opinion in Environmental Sustainability*, 42, pp. 15–21.

Chapter 6

1   Rescourio, A., & Tridimas, B. (2023, November 15). *Greta Thunberg's rise from youth activist to global climate leader | Context.* News Thomson Reuters Foundation News. https://news.trust.org/item/20190819233721-jaa90/

2   Tindall, D. (2020, October 6). *What lies ahead for fridays for future and the youth climate movement.* The Conversation. https://theconversation.com/what-lies-ahead-for-fridays-for-future-and-the-youth-climate-movement-147152

3   Han, H., & Ahn, S. W. (2020). "Youth mobilization to stop global climate change: Narratives and impact," *Sustainability*, 12(10), p. 4127.

4   XR (n.d.). *XR in your area.* Extinction Rebellion. https://rebellion.global/groups/#countries

5   Han, & Ahn, "Youth mobilization to stop global climate change," p. 4127.

6   *Who we are* (2023, September 25). Fridays for Future US. https://fridaysforfutureusa.org/

7   Volcovici, V. (2019, September 18). *Greta Thunberg to Congress: "Don't listen to me. Listen to the scientists."* Reuters. https://www.reuters.com/article/climate-change-thunberg-congress/update-1-greta-thunberg-to-congress-dont-listen-to-me-listen-to-the-scientists-idUSL2N2690MK

8   Wretched of the Earth (2019, May 4). *An open letter to extinction rebellion.* Common Dreams. https://www.commondreams.org/views/2019/05/04/open-letter-extinction-rebellion

9   Engels, A. (2019). "How should we ask questions about the social status of climate change knowledge?," *Wiley Interdisciplinary Reviews. Climate Change*, 10(4), p. e584.

10 Evensen, D. (2019). "The rhetorical limitations of the #FridaysForFuture movement," *Nature Climate Change*, 9(6), pp. 428–30.

11 Gardiner, S. (2016, January 9). *Why climate change is an ethical problem.* The Washington Post. https://www.washingtonpost.com/news/in-theory/wp/2016/01/09/why-climate-change-is-an-ethical-problem

12 Dotson, T. (2021). *The divide: How fanatical certitude is destroying democracy*. MIT Press.

13 Howe, N. (2020, November 3). "'Stick to the science': When science gets political," *Nature Podcast*. https://doi.org/10.1038/d41586-020-03067-w

14 Moore, J. W. (2017). "The Capitalocene, Part I: On the nature and origins of our ecological crisis," *The Journal of Peasant Studies*, 44(3), pp. 594–630.

15 United Nations (n.d.). *Vanessa Nakate: Climate change is about the people*. https://www.un.org/en/climatechange/vanessa-nakate-climate-change-is-about-people

16 *Young climate activists demand action and inspire hope*. (n.d.). UNICEF. https://www.unicef.org/stories/young-climate-activists-demand-action-inspire-hope

17 Markowitz, E. M. (2012). "Is climate change an ethical issue? Examining young adults' beliefs about climate and morality," *Climatic change*, 114(3–4), pp. 479–95.

18 Fridays for Future (2020, May 11). *Our demands*. https://fridaysforfuture.org/what-we-do/our-demands/

19 Marquardt, J. (2020). "Fridays for future's disruptive potential: An inconvenient youth between moderate and radical ideas," *Frontiers in Communication*, 5.

20 United Nations (n.d.). *The Paris agreement*. https://www.un.org/en/climatechange/paris-agreement

21 Berkeley Earth (2024, January 12). *2023 was warmest year since 1850*. https://berkeleyearth.org/press-release-2023-was-the-warmest-year-on-recordpress-release

22 Osaka, S. (2024, February 8). *Earth breached a feared level of warming over the past year. Are we doomed?* The Washington Post. www.washingtonpost.com/climate-environment/2024/02/08/1-5-celsius-global-warming-record/

23 Mooney, A. (2023, March 16). *Is 1.5C still realistic? The crumbling consensus over key climate target*. Financial Times. https://www.ft.com/content/450a59bb-7c83-4d04-851f-0bbc120c09f7

24   Democracy Now! (2015, December 14). *Protest in Paris: Climate justice activists decry accord as "Death sentence" for millions.* https://www. democracynow.org/2015/12/14/protest_in_paris_climate_justice_ activists

25   Torres, J. (2015, December 14). *Philippine activists decry Paris climate pact.* UCAnews.com. https://www.ucanews.com/news/philippine-activists-decry-paris-climate-pact/74784

26   Mundahl, E. (2017, November 19). *Native American environmental activists say Paris agreement doesn't go far enough.* InsideSources. https://insidesources.com/native-american-environmental-activists-say-paris-agreement-doesnt-go-far-enough/

27   Kusnetz, N. (2021, July 27). *Why the Paris climate agreement might be doomed to fail.* Inside Climate News. https://insideclimatenews.org/ news/28072021/pairs-agreement-success-failure/?gclid=CjwKCAjwlqO XBhBqEiwA-hhitO3F-VUahKkwzlQScu3ISiRJSTi839QF8vUxbV89W NjcqQrxH3y7xBoCMWcQAvD_BwE

28   Beslik, S. (2019, March 18). *5 Reasons why the Paris Agreement is a joke (and how we can fix it).* Medium. https://medium.com/in-search-of-leverage/5-reasons-why-the-paris-agreement-is-a-joke-and-how-we-can-fix-it-4b636409bb05

29   Michaelson, R. (2022, November 10). *"Explosion" in number of fossil fuel lobbyists at Cop27 climate summit.* The Guardian. https://www. theguardian.com/environment/2022/nov/10/big-rise-in-number-of-fossil-fuel-lobbyists-at-cop27-climate-summit

30   Lakhani, N. (2023, December 5). *Record number of fossil fuel lobbyists get access to Cop28 climate talks.* The Guardian. https://www. theguardian.com/environment/2023/dec/05/record-number-of-fossil-fuel-lobbyists-get-access-to-cop28-climate-talks

31   Bond, P., & D'Sa, D. (2021, November 15). *Glasgow's "Conference of the polluters" again confirms that global arson needs local fire extinguishers.* CADTM. https://www.cadtm.org/Glasgow-s-Conference-of-the-Polluters-again-confirms-that-global-arson-needs

32   Kennedy, R. (2021, November 9). *Climate activists decry "false solutions, fairy tales" at COP26.* Al Jazeera. https://www.aljazeera.com/

news/2021/11/9/climate-activists-decry-false-solutions-fairy-tales-at-cop26

33 Greenfield, P., & Kimeu, C. (2023, September 8). *Shell signals retreat from carbon offsetting.* The Guardian. https://www.theguardian.com/environment/2023/sep/08/shell-signals-retreat-from-carbon-offsetting

34 Greenfield, P. (2023, January 18). *Revealed: More than 90% of rainforest carbon offsets by biggest certifier are worthless, analysis shows.* The Guardian. https://www.theguardian.com/environment/2023/jan/18/revealed-forest-carbon-offsets-biggest-provider-worthless-verra-aoe

35 Miller, M. (2021, June 15). *Thunberg-linked climate movement disbands itself for being "racist."* The Washington Post. https://www.washingtonpost.com/world/2021/06/15/climate-change-racism-strike-greta-auckland/

36 Von Schermer, S. (2019, August 2). *Fridays for future: Die fast perfekte Jugendbewegung.* ZEIT Campus. https://www.zeit.de/campus/2019-07/fridays-for-future-sommerkongress-dortmund-klimawandel-aktivismus/komplettansicht?utm_referrer=https%3A%2F%2Fwww.frontiersin.org%2F

37 Marquardt, "Fridays for future's disruptive potential."

38 Chase, J. (2019, March 15). *Fridays for future: #Climatestrike comes of age.* DW. https://www.dw.com/en/fridays-for-future-the-climatestrike-movement-comes-of-age/a-47938623

39 Niranjan, A., Gayle, D., & Lakhani, N. (2023, December 7). *The war in Gaza has come for the climate movement.* Mother Jones. https://www.motherjones.com/politics/2023/12/greta-thunberg-gaza-war-israel-climate-movement-cop28/

40 Wallis, H., & Loy, L. S. (2021). "What drives pro-environmental activism of young people? A survey study on the Fridays for Future movement," *Journal of Environmental Psychology*, 74, p. 101581.

41 Marquardt, "Fridays for future's disruptive potential," 48.

42 XR-UK and XR-Global have slightly different but overlapping demands that have evolved over time. The demands we have paraphrased here are from the past. The current wording of the demands can be seen here: https://rebellion.global/; https://extinctionrebellion.uk/the-truth/demands/

43 XR (2023, June 15). *About us*. Extinction Rebellion UK. https://extinctionrebellion.uk/the-truth/about-us/

44 Hallam, R. (n.d.). *Mass rebellion: When common sense turns into rebellion*. Chelsea Green Publishing. https://www.chelseagreen.com/2019/when-common-sense-equals-mass-rebellion/

45 https://twitter.com/RogerHallamCS21/status/1180974430136209408 (Italics added for emphasis).

46 James, J. (2021, August 25). *The extinction rebellion protesters determined to bring London to a standstill*. My London. https://www.mylondon.news/news/zone-1-news/people-remember-heroes-extinction-rebellion-21397749

47 https://www.facebook.com/extinctionrebellionbirmingham

48 https://www.facebook.com/RichmondXR/posts/heroes-i-am-so-proud-of-our-tell-the-truth-tube-action-today-and-yesterday-four-/424052678222823/

49 Keighley, F. (2019, November 20). *Lord hain: We may look back on extinction rebellion as heroes*. London Press Club. https://londonpressclub.co.uk/?p=169

50 XR, *About us*.

51 Chenoweth, E. (2020). "Questions, answers, and some cautionary updates regarding the 3.5% rule," Harvard University, Carr Center Discussion Paper 5.

52 DeChristopher, T. (2020, May 13). *It's not as simple as rebellion*. YES! Magazine. https://www.yesmagazine.org/issue/coronavirus-community-power/2020/05/11/its-not-as-simple-as-rebellionn

53 DeChristopher, *It's not as simple as rebellion*.

54 https://www.facebook.com/events/d41d8cd9/xr-non-violent-direct-action-training-nvda-falmouth/495263154326561/

55 Lewis, A. (2019, November 24). *Too white, too middle class and lacking in empathy, extinction rebellion has a race problem, critics say*. CNN. https://www.cnn.com/2019/11/24/uk/extinction-rebellion-environment-diversity-gbr-intl/index.html

56 Woods, O. (2019, July 19). *Extinction rebellion: Not the struggle we need, Pt. 1*. libcom.org. https://libcom.org/article/extinction-rebellion-not-struggle-we-need-pt-1

57 Gayle, D. (2019, October 12). *Critics call out extinction rebellion's race problem*. Grist. https://grist.org/justice/critics-call-out-extinction-rebellions-race-problem/

58 Wretched of the Earth, *An open letter to extinction rebellion.*

59 Lewis, *Too white, too middle class and lacking in empathy, extinction rebellion has a race problem, critics say.*

60 Gayle, D. (2019, October 4). *Does extinction rebellion have a race problem?* The Guardian. https://www.theguardian.com/environment/2019/oct/04/extinction-rebellion-race-climate-crisis-inequality

61 O'Hare, M. (2022, July 4). *New law strengthen police powers on unauthorised encampments.* Nottinghamshire Live. https://www.nottinghampost.com/news/nottingham-news/what-new-police-crime-sentencing-7271483

62 BBC (2019, October 17). *Extinction rebellion protesters dragged from tube train roof.* https://www.bbc.com/news/uk-england-london-50079716

63 Zapata, N. (2020, October 5). *Extinction rebellion's long overdue reckoning with race.* The Nation. https://www.thenation.com/article/politics/extinction-rebellion-climate-race/

64 Gayle, D. (2021, April 1). *Critics call out extinction rebellion's race problem.* Grist. https://grist.org/justice/critics-call-out-extinction-rebellions-race-problem/

65 Dembicki, G. (2020, April 28). *A debate over racism has split one of the world's most famous climate groups.* VICE—VICE is the definitive guide to enlightening information. https://www.vice.com/en/article/jgey8k/a-debate-over-racism-has-split-one-of-the-worlds-most-famous-climate-groups

66 XR (2021, January 5). *What are citizens' assemblies.* Extinction Rebellion. https://rebellion.global/blog/2021/01/05/citizens-assembly-climate-change/

67 Gayle, *Critics call out extinction rebellion's race problem.*

68 Goldenberg, S. (2013, May 15). *Diplomatic cables reveal aggressive GM lobbying by US officials.* The Guardian. https://www.theguardian.com/environment/2013/may/15/diplomatic-cables-gm-lobbying-us

69   Falkner, R. (2007). "The global biotech food fight: Why the United States got it so wrong," *The Brown Journal of World Affairs*, 14(1), pp. 99–110.

70   Buis, A. (2019, June 19). *A degree of concern: Why global temperatures matter—Climate change: Vital signs of the planet*. NASA. https://climate.nasa.gov/news/2865/a-degree-of-concern-why-global-temperatures-matter/

71   Taylor, M. (2020, August 4). *The evolution of extinction rebellion.* The Guardian. https://www.theguardian.com/environment/2020/aug/04/evolution-of-extinction-rebellion-climate-emergency-protest-coronavirus-pandemic

72   Dembicki, *A debate over racism has split one of the world's most famous climate groups.*

73   Woods, *Extinction rebellion.*

74   Lewis, *Too white, too middle class and lacking in empathy, extinction rebellion has a race problem, critics say.*

75   Gayle, *Does extinction rebellion have a race problem?*

76   XR (2020, July 1). *Statement on extinction rebellion's relationship with the police.* Extinction Rebellion UK. https://extinctionrebellion.uk/2020/07/01/statement-on-extinction-rebellions-relationship-with-the-police/

77   Zapata, *Extinction rebellion's long overdue reckoning with race.*

78   Rigitano, E. (2018, December 17). *COP24, the speech by 15-year-old climate activist Greta Thunberg everyone should listen to.* LifeGate. https://www.lifegate.com/greta-thunberg-speech-cop24

79   Buis, *A degree of concern.*

80   https://twitter.com/Fridays4future/status/1395111918898016259?ref_src=twsrc%5Etfw

81   Marri, N. (2024, January 22). *Greta Thunberg highlights seven-decade oppression of Baloch in Pakistan.* The Baloch Circle. https://thebalochcircle.com/greta-thunberg-highlights-seven-decade-oppression-of-baloch-in-pakistan/

82   https://twitter.com/FFFIndia/status/1515687703337406468

83   Lambert, X. (2009). "Sign the petition," *Vital*, 7, pp. 5. https://doi.org/10.1038/vital1066.

84 Janata Weekly. (2021, March 21). "Climate Justice Is about Intersectional Equality": Disha Ravi's First Statement after Arrest. https://janataweekly.org/climate-justice-is-about-intersectional-equality-disha-ravis-first-statement-after-arrest/.

85 Fisher, D. R., Berglund, O., & Davis, C. J. (2023). "How effective are climate protests at swaying policy—and what could make a difference?," *Nature*, 623(7989), pp. 910–13.

Chapter 7

1 Tuck, E., & Yang, K. Wayne (2012). "Decolonization is not a metaphor," *Decolonization: Indigeneity, Education & Society*, 1, p. 1–40.

2 Ghosh, A. (2022). *The nutmeg's curse: Parables for a planet in crisis.* John Murray.

3 Bhambra, G. K., & Newell, P. (2022). "More than a metaphor: 'Climate colonialism' in perspective," *Global Social Challenges Journal*, 1, pp. 1–9.

4 Miles, K. (2018, October 9). *Ecofeminism.* Encyclopedia Britannica. https://www.britannica.com/topic/ecofeminism

5 Nixon, L. (2015, April 30). *Eco-feminist appropriations of Indigenous feminisms and environmental violence.* The Feminist Wire. https://thefeministwire.com/2015/04/eco-feminist-appropriations-of-indigenous-feminisms-and-environmental-violence

6 Sargisson, L. (2001). "What's wrong with ecofeminism," *Environmental Politics*, 10(1), pp. 52–64.

7 MacGregor, S. (2021). "Making matter great again? Ecofeminism, new materialism and the everyday turn in environmental politics," *Environmental Politics*, 30(1–2), pp. 41–60.

8 Maria, M., & Shiva, V. (1993). *Ecofeminism.* Zed Books.

9 Nyamweru, C. (2003). "Women and the sacred groves in coastal Kenya: A contribution to the ecofeminist debate," in *Ecofeminism & Globalization: Exploring Culture, Context, and Religion.* Rowman & Littlefield.

10   Gabriele, D. (1992). *Reflections on the women's movement in India: Religion ecology development*. Horizon India Books; Gnanadason, A. (2003). "Traditions of prudence lost: A tragic world of broken relationships," in *Ecofeminism & globalization: Exploring culture, context, and religion*. Rowman & Littlefield.

11   Hasnain, A., & Srivastava, A. (2023). "Vegetarianism without vegetarians: Caste ideology and the politics of food in India," *Food & Foodways*, 31(4), pp. 273–95.

12   The Nobel Prize (2004, October 8). *Press Release*. NobelPrize.org. https://www.nobelprize.org/prizes/peace/2004/press-release/

13   Ighobor, K. (2012, September 20). *Wangari Maathai, the woman of trees, dies*. Africa Renewal. https://www.un.org/africarenewal/web-features/wangari-maathai-woman-trees-dies

14   Hunt, Kathleen P. (2014). "'It's more than planting trees, it's planting ideas': Ecofeminist praxis in the Green Belt Movement," *Southern Communication Journal*, 79, p. 235.

15   Kings, A. E. (2017). "Intersectionality and the changing face of ecofeminism," *Ethics and the Environment*, 22(1), p. 63.

16   Lloro-Bidart, T., & Finewood, M. H. (2018). "Intersectional feminism for the environmental studies and sciences: Looking inward and outward," *Journal of Environmental Studies and Sciences*, 8, pp. 142–51.

17   Sturgeon, N. L. (2009). *Environmentalism in popular culture: Gender, race, sexuality, and the politics of the natural*. University of Arizona Press.

18   Kashwan, P. (2021, January 7). *Rights of nature*. Outlook India. https://www.outlookindia.com/opinion/india-news-rights-of-nature-news-304135

19   hooks, b. (1985). *Feminist theory from margin to center*. South End Press; hooks, b. (2009). *Belonging: A culture of place*. Routledge.

20   James, Jennifer C. (2022). "A theory of the bottom: Black ecofeminism as politics," *Resilience: A Journal of the Environmental Humanities*, 10(1), pp. 46–52.

21   hooks, *Belonging*.

22   Cited in: James, "A theory of the bottom," 46–52.

23 Freire, P. (2018). *Pedagogy of the oppressed: 50th anniversary edition.*
    4th ed. Bloomsbury Academic.

24 Buchanan, L., Bui, Q., & Patel, J. (2020, July 3). *Black Lives Matter may
    be the largest movement in U.S. history.* The New York Times. https://
    www.nytimes.com/interactive/2020/07/03/us/george-floyd-protests-
    crowd-size.html

25 Bhambhani, D. (2016, February 10). PR Week. https://www.prweek.com/
    article/1383011/communications-goals-strategies-black-lives-matter

26 Dillon, L., & Sze, J. (2016). "Police power and particulate matters:
    Environmental justice and the spatialities of in/securities in US cities,"
    English Language Notes, 54(2), pp. 13–23.

27 C3JN (2020, June). *Letter of support and solidarity re: Black Lives
    Matter.* Environmental Justice / Climate Justice Hub | Orfalea Center
    for Global & International Studies. https://ejcj.orfaleacenter.ucsb.edu/
    black-lives-matter/

28 Mathiesen, K. (2014, April 7). *Defining moments in climate change:
    Hope and crisis in Copenhagen.* The Guardian. https://www.
    theguardian.com/global-development-professionals-network/2014/
    apr/07/copenhagen-climate-change-paris-talks

29 Sealey-Huggins, Leon (2018). "The climate crisis is a racist crisis:
    structural racism, inequality and climate change," in Johnson, A.,
    Joseph-Salisbury, R., & Kamunge, B. (eds.) *The fire now: Anti-
    racist scholarship in times of explicit racial violence.* Zed Books,
    pp. 99–113.

30 Dickie, G. (2023, November 20). *Climate on track to warm by nearly
    3C without aggressive actions, UN report finds.* Reuters. https://www.
    reuters.com/sustainability/climate-energy/climate-track-warm-by-
    nearly-3c-without-greater-ambition-un-report-2023-11-20/

31 Tutu, D. (2014, April 10). *We need an apartheid-style boycott to
    save the planet.* The Guardian. https://www.theguardian.com/
    commentisfree/2014/apr/10/divest-fossil-fuels-climate-change-
    keystone-xll

32 Global Fossil Fuel Divestment Commitments Database. https://
    divestmentdatabase.org/

33   Cojoianu, T. F., Ascui, F., Clark, G. L., Hoepner, A. G., & Wójcik, D. (2021). "Does the fossil fuel divestment movement impact new oil and gas fundraising?" *Journal of Economic Geography*, 21(1), pp. 141–64.

34   Chakrabarty, D. (2018). "Planetary crises and the difficulty of being modern," *Millennium*, 46(3), pp. 259–82.

35   Ayling, J., & Gunningham, N. (2017). "Non-state governance and climate policy: the fossil fuel divestment movement," *Climate Policy*, 17(2), pp. 131–49.

36   Hestres, L. E., & Hopke, J. E. (2020). "Fossil fuel divestment: Theories of change, goals, and strategies of a growing climate movement," *Environmental Politics*, 29(3), pp. 371–89.

37   Curwood, S. (2020, July 9). *Bill McKibben on the divestment movement*. The Allegheny Front. https://www.alleghenyfront.org/bill-mckibben-on-the-divestment-movement; Stanley, M. (n.d.). *Climate change and fossil fuel aware investing*. https://www.morganstanley.com/pub/content/dam/msdotcom/articles/fossil-fuels/Climate-Change-Fossil-Fuel-Aware-Investing_Primer

38   Shell (2017). *Shell annual report 2017*. https://reports.shell.com/annual-report/2017/

39   The Movement for Black Lives (2021, February 1). *Invest-divest*. M4BL. https://m4bl.org/policy-platforms/invest-divest/

40   Cohen, I. (2020, June 20). *Chevron's "Black Lives Matter" tweet prompts a debate about big oil and environmental justice*. Inside Climate News. https://insideclimatenews.org/news/20062020/chevron-black-lives-matter-twitter/

41   Mangat, R., Dalby, S., & Paterson, M. (2018). "Divestment discourse: War, justice, morality and money," *Environmental Politics*, 27(2), pp. 187–208. https://doi.org/10.1080/09644016.2017.1413725

42   Fossil Free Campaign (n.d.). *About Us*. https://gofossilfree.org/about/

43   Bob E., & Ladd A. E. (2000). "Environmental justice, swine production and farm loss in North Carolina," *Sociological Spectrum: The Official Journal of the Mid-South Sociological Association*, 20(3), pp. 263–90; Taylor, D. E. (2011). "Introduction: The evolution of environmental

justice activism, research, and scholarship," *Environmental Practice: Journal of the National Association of Environmental Professionals,* 13(4), pp. 280–301.

44 Lederer, E. (2024, February 14). *UN chief warns climate chaos and food crises threaten global peace: "Empty bellies fuel unrest."* PBS. https://www.pbs.org/newshour/world/un-chief-warns-climate-chaos-and-food-crises-threaten-global-peace-empty-bellies-fuel-unrest

45 Cohn, C., & Duncanson, C. (2022, October 12). *Securitizing climate change: How to not think about the climate crisis.* IPI Global Observatory. https://theglobalobservatory.org/2022/10/securitizing-climate-change-how-to-not-think-about-the-climate-crisis/

46 BioVision (2023, August 15). Agroecology info pool. https://www.agroecology-pool.org/agroecology/

47 Calvário, R., & Desmarais, A. A. (2023). "The feminist dimensions of food sovereignty: Insights from La Via Campesina's politics," *The Journal of Peasant Studies,* 50(2), pp. 640–64.

48 Holt-Gimenez, E. (2015). *Review of the Campesino a Campesino Movement: Linking sustainable agriculture and social change.* Institute For Food & Development Policy. https://foodfirst.org/the-campesino-a-campesino-movement/

49 Val, V., Rosset, P. M., Zamora Lomelí, C., Giraldo, O. F., & Rocheleau, D. (2019). "Agroecology and la via Campesina I. The symbolic and material construction of agroecology through the dispositive of "peasant-to-peasant" processes," *Agroecology and Sustainable Food Systems,* 43(7–8), pp. 872–94. https://doi.org/10.1080/21683565.2019.1600099

50 La Via Campesina (n.d.). *International peasants' movement.* https://viacampesina.org/en

51 La Via Campesina (2022, June 7). *Celebrating thirty years of our struggles: Sharing and reflecting our struggles towards food sovereignty in the southern and eastern Africa.* La Via Campesina. https://viacampesina.org/en/celebrating-30-years-of-our-struggles-sharing-and-reflecting-our-struggles-towards-food-sovereignty-in-the-southern-and-eastern-africa/

52   Peña, D., Calvo, L., McFarland, P., & Valle, G. R. (eds.) (2017). *Mexican-origin foods, foodways, and social movements: Decolonial perspectives*. University of Arkansas Press.

53   Borras Jr. S.M. (2008). "La Vía Campesina and its global campaign for agrarian reform," *Journal of Agrarian Change*, 8(2–3), pp. 258–89.

54   Kashwan, Prakash (2017). *Democracy in the woods: Environmental conservation and social justice in India, Tanzania, and Mexico*. Oxford University Press.

55   Edelman, M., & Borras, S. M. (2016). "Prelims—Political dynamics of transnational agrarian movements," *Political Dynamics of Transnational Agrarian Movements*, i–xxii. https://doi.org/10.3362/9781780449142.000

56   Edelman, & Borras, "Prelims—Political dynamics of transnational agrarian movements," pp. i–xxii.

57   Montenegro de Wit, M., Canfield, M., Iles, A., Anderson, M., McKeon, N., Guttal, S., Gemmill-Herren, B., Duncan, J., van der Ploeg, J.D., & Prato, S. (2021). "Resetting power in global food governance: The UN Food Systems Summit," *Development*, 64, pp. 153–61.

58   Clark, C. (2023, August 23). *Buffalo slaughter left lasting impact on Indigenous Peoples*. Emory News Center. https://news.emory.edu/stories/2023/08/esc_bison_impact_24-08-2023/story.html

59   Bullard, R. D. (ed.) (1992). *Confronting environmental racism: Voices from the grassroots*. South End Press; Cole, L. W., & Foster, S. R. (2020). *From the ground up: Environmental racism and the rise of the environmental justice movement*. New York University Press.

60   Estes, N. (2019). *Our history is the future: Standing rock versus the Dakota access pipeline, and the long tradition of Indigenous resistance*. Verso Books. Gilio-Whitaker, D. (2019). *As long as grass grows: The Indigenous fight for environmental justice, from colonization to Standing Rock*. Beacon Press.

61   Gilio-Whitaker, D. (2022, July 1). *Environmental justice is only the beginning*. High Country News. https://www.hcn.org/issues/54.7/indigenous-affairs-perspective-environmental-justice-is-only-the-beginning

62 Estes, *Our history is the future.*

63 Erdrich, L. (2016, December 22). *Holy rage: Lessons from standing rock.* The New Yorker. https://www.newyorker.com/news/news-desk/holy-rage-lessons-from-standing-rock

64 New Day Films (2018). *Water warriors: A community's resistance against the oil & gas industry.*

65 Lakota People's Law Project (2020, August 14). *#LandBack is climate justice.* https://lakotalaw.org/news/2020-08-14/land-back-climate-justice

66 Latulippe, N., & Klenk, N. (2020). "Making room and moving over: Knowledge co-production, Indigenous knowledge sovereignty and the politics of global environmental change decision-making," *Current Opinion in Environmental Sustainability*, 42, pp. 7–14.

67 Gilio-Whitaker, D. (2019, July 10). *How to indigenize the Green New Deal and environmental justice.* High Country News. https://www.hcn.org/articles/tribal-affairs-how-to-indigenize-the-green-new-deal-and-environmental-justice/

68 Thompson, V. D. *et al.* (2020). "Ecosystem stability and Native American oyster harvesting along the Atlantic Coast of the United States," *Science Advances*, 6(28), p. eaba9652.

69 Yazzie, Melanie K. (2018). "Decolonizing development in Diné Bikeyah: Resource extraction, anti-capitalism, and relational futures," *Environment and Society*, 9, pp. 25–39.

70 Whyte K. (2020). "Too late for indigenous climate justice: Ecological and relational tipping points." *WIREs Clim Change*, 11, p. e603. https://doi.org/10.1002/wcc.603.

71 SEAS (2022, June 30). *Four questions: Professor Kyle Whyte.* University of Michigan School for Environment and Sustainability. https://www.seas.umich.edu/news/four-questions-seas-professor-kyle-whyte

72 Klein, N., & Feeney, L. (2018, March 20). *Puerto Ricans and Ultrarich "Puertopians" are locked in a pitched struggle over how to remake the island.* The Intercept. https://theintercept.com/2018/03/20/puerto-rico-hurricane-maria-recovery/

73 Kashwan, P. (2023). "Globalization of environmental justice: A framework for comparative research," in Sowers, J., VanDeveer, S. D., & Weinthal, E. (eds.) *The Oxford handbook of comparative environmental politics*. Oxford University Press, pp. 475–98.

74 Ranganathan, M. (2022). "Caste, racialization, and the making of environmental unfreedoms in urban India," *Ethnic & Racial Studies*, 45(2), pp. 43–63.

75 Otero, G. (2004). "Global economy, local politics: Indigenous struggles, civil society and democracy," *Canadian Journal of Political Science/ Revue canadienne de science politique*, 37(2), pp. 325–46.

76 Polanyi, K. (2001[1957]). *The great transformation: The political and economic origins of our time*. Beacon Press; Fraser, N. (2017). "Beyond neoliberalism : Social analysis after 1989," in *A triple movement? parsing the politics of crisis after Polanyi*. Springer International Publishing; Palgrave Macmillan, p. 29. Essay Burchardt Marian. burchardt@mmg.mpg.de, Max Planck Institute for the Study of Religious and Ethnic Diversity Göttingen Germany.

77 Fanon, F. (1961). *The Wretched of the earth*. Grove Press, p. 24.

Index